TYRANNY
OF THE
STATUS QUO

TYRANNY OF THE STATUS QUO

MILTON & ROSE FRIEDMAN

HARCOURT BRACE JOVANOVICH, PUBLISHERS
San Diego   New York   London

Excerpt from *Before the Fall* by William Safire. Copyright © 1975 by William Safire. Reprinted by permission of Doubleday & Company, Inc.
Excerpt from "Tax Follies of 1970," by Milton Friedman, in *Newsweek* magazine, April 27, 1970. Copyright © by Newsweek Inc. All rights reserved. Reprinted by permission.
Excerpt from "Congress and the Federal Reserve," by Milton Friedman, in *Newsweek* magazine, June 2, 1975. Copyright © 1975 by Newsweek Inc. All rights reserved. Reprinted by permission.
Excerpt from "More Double Talk at the Fed," by Milton Friedman, in *Newsweek* magazine, May 2, 1983. Copyright © 1983 by Newsweek, Inc. All rights reserved. Reprinted by permission.
Excerpt from *The Law and the Profits* by C. Northcote Parkinson. Copyright © 1960 by C. Northcote Parkinson. Reprinted by permission of Houghton Mifflin Company and John Murray (Publishers) Ltd.
William H. Bell, Letter to the Editor, *Wall Street Journal*, July 25, 1983. Reprinted by permission.

Library of Congress Cataloging in Publication Data
Friedman, Milton, 1912–
Tyranny of the status quo.
Includes bibliographic references and index.
1. United States—Economic policy—1981–
2. Fiscal policy—United States.   3. Government spending policy—United States.   4. Deficit financing—United States.   I. Friedman, Rose D.   II. Title.
HC106.8.F74 1984   330.973'0927   83-22637
ISBN 0-15-192379-5

Designed by Dalia Hartman
Printed in the United States of America
First edition

To WJ
a friend, counselor, and critic extraordinaire

CONTENTS

1

THE REAGAN RECORD: PROMISE AND PERFORMANCE

We must move boldly, decisively and quickly to control the runaway growth of federal spending, to remove the tax disincentives that are throttling the economy, and to reform the regulatory web that is smothering it.

We must keep the rate of growth of government spending at reasonable and prudent levels.

We must reduce personal income tax rates and accelerate and simplify depreciation schedules in an orderly, systematic way to remove disincentives to work, savings, investment, and productivity.

We must review regulations that affect the economy, and change them to encourage growth.

We must establish a stable, sound, and predictable monetary policy.

—Ronald Reagan, September 9, 1980

IN THE FIRST MONTHS after his election, Ronald Reagan made real progress on some campaign promises, particularly those that required neither the approval of Congress nor actions by independent agencies such as the Federal Reserve System.

He promptly removed the legal ceiling on the price of oil and eliminated oil allocation controls. The results confounded his critics. They had argued that eliminating price ceilings on oil would lead to a sharp rise in the price of gasoline and other petroleum products. The actual result was the reverse. Deregulation freed the market and was followed by a decline in the price of oil.

The President was only slightly less successful in stemming a flood of regulations that had been pouring from various governmental departments in the final months of the Carter Administration. New regulations issued were cut by one third, and new administrative procedures were introduced that provided more careful review of proposed regulations. The Federal Register has continued to fatten—but at a far slower pace than before.

The President has much less power over government spending and taxes than over regulatory procedures. Nonetheless, President Reagan had remarkable initial success in persuading Congress to adopt his proposals for taxes and spending, even if in somewhat revised form. The Congress in 1981 (1) reduced tax rates by 25 percent over a three-year period, (2) provided for the indexation of taxes in 1985, and (3) reduced the top income tax rate from 70 to 50 percent immediately. It also legislated cuts in government spending in many areas, as well as a substantial increase in funds for defense.

This was Reagan's honeymoon. It lasted about six to nine months. Then the tyranny of the status quo asserted itself. Every special interest that was threatened proceeded to mount a campaign to prevent its particular governmental sinecure from being eliminated. Government spending continued to rise as a fraction of income *even after allowing for the expenditures associated with recession.* Government taxes stayed almost the same as a fraction of income because legislated tax cuts were offset by a rise in Social Security taxes and by "bracket creep" as a result of inflation. Then in 1982 there was a legislated rise in taxes. Even in the area of regulation, deregulation slowed and was reversed in some areas.

Nonetheless, there was a vast difference in the general atmosphere under which policy was being conducted. Every earlier recession of comparable scope had generated an immediate flood of government spending proposals alleged "to create jobs." During 1981 and early 1982, talk abounded about similar programs, but few major proposals for large-scale job-creating programs were considered seriously. Not until late 1982, when the recession had just about run its course, did a so-called jobs bill finally get through Congress. But that bill was far smaller in size than similar measures passed during earlier recessions.

President Reagan's experience conforms to a political generalization that has repeatedly proved valid: a new administration has some six to nine months in which to achieve major changes; if it does not seize the opportunity to act decisively during that period, it will not have another such opportunity. Further changes come slowly or not at all, and counterattacks develop against the initial changes. The temporarily routed political forces regroup, and they tend to mobilize everyone who was adversely affected by the changes, while the proponents of the changes tend to relax after their initial victories.

This generalization has a corollary: a candidate for head of state who hopes to make a real difference has to do more than get elected; he or she must have a detailed program of action well worked out before the election. If a new head of state waits until after the election to convert a general policy position into a detailed program, the program will be ready too late to get adopted.

If the early successes of a new administration reflect a basic change in public opinion, the apparent lack of further progress after the first six to nine months will be deceptive. The early actions will continue to have their effects after they have disappeared from the front pages. The altered political atmosphere will lead the defeated opposition to modify its political position. Even if the opposition succeeds in returning to power, it will not pursue the same course that it pursued before.

The New Deal administration of Franklin Delano Roosevelt is an almost perfect textbook example. He was swept into office on a tidal change in public opinion produced by the Great Depression. He brought with him to Washington a "brains trust" that had been developing detailed proposals for change. The major New Deal social and economic measures were adopted in the famous "one hundred days" special session of Congress that Roosevelt called immediately after his inauguration. Just listing a few of the agencies that grew out of the legislation adopted during that session gives a taste of the scope of the changes:

AAA   Agricultural Adjustment Administration
CCC   Civilian Conservation Corps
CWA   Civilian Works Administration
FDIC   Federal Deposit Insurance Corporation
FERA   Federal Emergency Relief Administration
NRA   National Recovery Administration
PWA   Public Works Administration

Then change slowed, and when the Supreme Court declared AAA and NRA unconstitutional, some programs were eliminated—at least for a time, until they were revived under a different guise. Roosevelt tried to overcome this check by "packing" the Supreme Court but failed to persuade an overwhelmingly Democratic Congress. However, the structural changes set in train continued to alter the political and economic landscape. The Republican party, after a disastrous defeat in the 1936 presidential election—when it carried only Maine and Vermont—changed its character. The so-called Eastern wing became dominant, and it adopted much of the New Deal doctrine as its own. As a result, when the Republicans finally won the White House under Dwight D. Eisenhower in 1952, the move toward ever bigger and more centralized government continued, though under the Republicans the pace was slowed.

Within the past five years, not only the United States but also Britain, France, and Germany have seen a change in their heads of state that involved a decided change in political philosophy. In Britain in 1979, the Labourite James Callaghan lost to Conservative Margaret Thatcher; in France in 1981, the Independent Republican Valéry Giscard d'Estaing lost to Socialist François Mitterrand; recently, in Germany in 1983, the Social Democrat Helmut Schmidt lost to Christian Democrat Helmut Kohl.

The experience of Thatcher and Mitterrand, like that of Reagan, conforms to our generalization on the six-month "window" open to change, and their experience also illustrates the corollary that a new head of state must begin with detailed programs.

In her first months in office, Mrs. Thatcher succeeded in ending forty years of foreign exchange control, reducing the top income tax rate from 90 to 60 percent, denationalizing trucking, and adopting a "medium term financial strategy" to reduce monetary growth. Since then, these changes continue to have their effects, but there have been no further major moves. On the contrary, despite her emphasis on cutting the size of government, spending and taxes have both risen rather than fallen as a fraction of national income. Further moves toward denationalization and deregulation have been minor. Her recent reelection now gives her another chance. Once again, the first six to nine months will prove crucial. Further moves to shape British policy in accordance with Margaret Thatcher's beliefs in free markets and private enterprise will be made then—or not at all.

Mitterrand's experience demonstrates that the tyranny of the status quo plays no political favorites. In his first months in office, he raised the minimum wage, nationalized private banks and other enterprises, raised taxes and spending, and increased controls over prices and wages. Since then, he has not been able to nail down other planks in his far-reaching socialist program. On the contrary, he has been forced to make a dramatic U-turn—adopting policies of restraint and austerity that bear the stamp of Margaret Thatcher and Ronald Reagan rather than Karl Marx and John Maynard Keynes.

Mitterrand's experience differs from Thatcher's and Reagan's for two reasons. His initial measures flew in the face of economic reality. Faced with high inflation and high unemployment, he took measures that could only make matters worse on both counts. The disastrous results of his initial measures were dramatized by three devaluations of the franc within two years. Second, and no less important, public opinion did not support his move toward more radical socialism. Insofar as there had been any change in public opinion in France, it was, as in other countries, in the opposite direction—toward conservatism.

A recent election in a Canadian province illustrates our generalization in a rather different way—one that brings out clearly a major reason why the generalization is valid and also bears particularly on the prospects after reelection. William R. Bennett was recently reelected for his third term as premier of British Columbia. Immediately after his reelection, he announced a sweeping program to reduce the role of the provincial government: he proposed to cut the number of government employees by 25 percent and to reduce spending on a wide range of programs. In addition, he abolished outright a number of politically sensitive commissions. There has understandably been an outcry of rage and frustration from threatened civil servants and other groups directly affected by his actions.

Now, Mr. Bennett could have introduced these measures before the election instead of immediately thereafter. Why didn't he? The answer is so obvious that it is embarrassing to spell it out, yet it is crucial to understanding the generalization with which we started and the parallel tyranny of the status quo. Any measure that affects a *concentrated* group significantly—either favorably or unfavorably—tends to have effects on individual members of that group that are substantial, occur promptly, and are highly visible. The effects of the same measure on the individual members of a *diffused* group—again whether favorable or unfavorable—tend to be trivial, longer delayed, and less visible. Quick, concentrated reaction is the major source of the strength of special interest groups in a democracy—or for that matter any other kind of government. It motivates politicians to make grandiose promises to such special interests before an election—and to postpone any measures adversely affecting special interest groups until after an election.

Had Premier Bennett spelled out his intention to cut personnel and funds before the election, he would have aroused immediate and vocal opposition from the special interest groups affected—and only lukewarm and far less vocal enthusiasm from the taxpayers in general. By waiting until after the election to spell out his program, Premier Bennett could hope that the bad effects on the concentrated groups would dissipate before the next election while the good effects on a broad constituency would have time both to take effect and to be recognized as the result of the measures he took.

It may well be that a majority of the electorate—if well informed —would approve the measures before, as well as after, the election. But the minorities specially affected have strong incentives to mount a propaganda barrage to assure that the majority are not well informed, and their task is easier than that of their opponents. They have visible, immediate effects to portray; their opponents, indirect delayed effects.

To return to the effect of Ronald Reagan's election as President, the ultimate effect depends on whether, like Roosevelt and Thatcher, he is supported by a basic change in public opinion or, like Mitterrand, he is not. In our earlier book, *Free to Choose*, published in early 1980, we wrote:

> The failure of Western governments to achieve their proclaimed objectives has produced a widespread reaction against big government. . . .
>
> The reaction may prove short-lived and be followed, after a brief interval, by a resumption of the trend toward ever bigger government. The widespread enthusiasm for reducing government taxes and other impositions is not matched by a comparable enthusiasm for eliminating government programs—except programs that benefit other people. The reaction against big government has been sparked by rampant inflation which governments can control if they find it politically profitable to do so. If they do, the reaction might be muted or disappear.
>
> We believe that the reaction is more than a response to transitory inflation. . . . (p. 283)

The election of Ronald Reagan to the presidency in November 1980 seemed to us further confirmation that "The Tide Is Turning," as we titled the final chapter of *Free to Choose*. Ronald Reagan was elected not because he had adjusted his views to what the voters wanted to hear but because the public had come to accept the views he had been expressing for nearly two decades. For most of this period, it was political suicide for any politician to campaign for national office on the basis of such views.

It has often been noted that the governmental structure in the United States makes it very difficult to achieve change except at a time of major crisis. The Great Depression culminating in the banking holiday in March 1933 was such a crisis. In time of war, similar governmental initiatives are possible. But under ordinary circumstances, the complex division of power introduced into our Constitution by its framers—the division between federal and state governments, the balance among the legislative, the executive, and the judiciary, between the two houses of the Congress—all these have made the process of producing substantial change both difficult and lengthy.

Commentators have often compared the structure in the United States unfavorably with the parliamentary structure in countries such as Britain, in which there is a "government" that can specify policy and have it carried out almost immediately. When a British Prime Minister proposes a budget to the Parliament, that budget becomes law unless the Parliament passes a vote of no confidence—which leads to the dissolution of that Parliament and the staging of new elections. When a United States President proposes a budget, that is simply the starting point for extensive and almost continuous debate. Any resemblance between his proposal and the final budget may be purely coincidental.

We have ourselves always regarded the American structure as a virtue, not a vice. While it is certainly harder to make good changes in our system than in a parliamentary system, it is also harder to make bad changes. Britain moved much more rapidly than the United States down the road to the welfare state largely because of this difference in governmental structure. Conversely, the United States can move away from the welfare state less rapidly than Britain has under

Mrs. Thatcher. However, *we also have less far to go and, as we move, what we do will be more difficult to undo.* Like God's mill, public opinion "grinds slow, but sure."

Like Margaret Thatcher, Ronald Reagan may have a second chance to make major changes. If he does have that chance, he will do well to ponder what we regard as the major mistake of his first term: his failure to take full advantage of the initial brief window of time for which the tyranny of the status quo was suspended. He made what seemed like bold proposals and succeeded in getting much of what he asked for. But his proposals were not bold enough. He would have received no more criticism, then or subsequently, if he had made much bolder, more far-reaching proposals for cutting government spending and eliminating harmful government programs—proposals that if adopted would in fact have led to the balanced budget by 1984 that he promised during his campaign. He would not have succeeded in getting all he asked for—but he would have gotten much more than he did, and we would now be farther ahead on the road toward achieving his basic objectives.

If Ronald Reagan runs for a second term and is reelected, the tyranny of the status quo will again be suspended for a few months. With inflation subdued even if not yet conquered, he will be able to take additional major steps to curb the growth of government and expand the freedom of the citizens—provided that he prepares detailed plans in advance to be implemented and recommended to Congress promptly once he is reelected, provided those plans are bold enough, and provided he resists the temptation to make promises in the course of the campaign that are inconsistent with his basic philosophy.

This book surveys the progress—and lack of progress—during the first two and a half years of Ronald Reagan's presidency in reducing the size of government and transferring functions from the federal to state governments and from both to the citizen. It examines the obstacles that have slowed that progress and that threaten to block further progress. And finally, it suggests ways in which we can overcome those obstacles.

We have no easy formula to offer. But we retain our confidence that once the American people understand the problem, they will be able to control their government and shape it in accordance with their continuing desire that America remain the land of freedom and of promise.

2

THE FACTS:
GOVERNMENT SPENDING,
TAXES, AND DEFICITS

We must keep the rate of growth of government spending at reasonable and prudent levels.

We must balance the budget, reduce tax rates, and restore our defenses.

—Ronald Reagan, September 9, 1980

WE SUGGEST that you conduct a simple personal experiment. Add up the taxes that you are reasonably aware of having paid in 1982: personal income taxes—state, federal, and local—and the Social Security tax that are deducted from your paycheck, the property tax on your home, the sales tax on your retail purchases, the tax on gasoline, the taxes on your telephone bill, and any other assorted taxes that you pay directly. If you are an average, representative taxpayer of the United States, that total will come to more than $2,500 for each person in your household—or more than $10,000 for the typical four-person family of husband, wife, and two children.

That sum only begins to measure how much government is costing you. In the first place, those taxes finance less than 60 percent of total government spending at all levels. Governments get the rest of their money from three sources: (1) taxes that most individuals are not aware of—taxes paid by corporations, customs duties, and a good many other miscellaneous imposts; (2) creating money out of worthless paper; (3) borrowing from the public in a wide variety of forms.

But do not be fooled. These "other" taxes are also laid on you! We always bear the cost. Businesses, whether incorporated or not, do not pay taxes. They simply serve as unappointed tax collectors. The taxes they transmit to the government can come only from their customers or their workers or their owners or their shareholders. And that is true whether the tax is called a corporate income tax or a windfall profits tax or a tariff or an excise tax—or by any other name.

Similarly, what is called a deficit is an even more subtle hidden tax, whether it is financed by pieces of paper or bookkeeping entries called money or by pieces of paper or bookkeeping entries called notes or bills or bonds. During the year ended September 30, 1982, the federal government spent $746 billion and took in $618 billion in what were called budget receipts. Who do you suppose paid the $128 billion difference, labeled a "deficit"? There is no Dutch uncle—not even an Uncle Sam—to pay it. We all pay, one way or the other.

Deficit financing also has a major political cost. It enables our legislative representatives to vote for expenditures that their constituents want without having to vote for the taxes to pay for them. "Who benefits" is something that legislators are delighted to stress. "Who pays" is something they prefer not to have to talk about. If Congress were required to balance the budget, this shell game would end.

If the government finances its deficit by creating money, it imposes a hidden tax of inflation—each dollar you have will buy less. In addition, inflation raises the amount that government collects through open taxes. Income taxes go up more than in proportion to inflation because increases in income that just match inflation push the taxpayer into higher income tax brackets subject to higher tax rates—the phenomenon that has been termed bracket creep. Excise and sales taxes go up roughly in proportion to inflation. The net result is that government gets additional funds without any new taxes having to be legislated.

If the government finances its deficit by borrowing, it gets funds that would otherwise be available for building houses or factories or machines. In the process, it assumes a heavier burden of interest payments, so that we can confidently look forward to higher taxes—both open and hidden—in the future.

However the government gets the money it spends, the goods and services that it buys, or that are bought by the people to whom it transfers money, are thereby not available for other use. *Those goods and services—not the pieces of paper that pay for them—are the real cost of government to the taxpayers.*

Even these goods and services do not measure in full what our government really costs us. Many costs that we bear as a result of government action are not recorded in the books of government as either spending or taxing. An obvious example is the time that we spend preparing our personal income tax returns or the money that we spend to hire others to do so. *That* surely is a cost of government that we pay even though it never enters the government's books.

In a 1970 *Newsweek* column, one of us estimated that

the total time [spent on preparing personal income tax returns] amounted to the horrendous total of 300 million man hours, or the equivalent of 150,000 men working 40 hours a week for 50 weeks a year—and this does not include the time spent by employees of business enterprises in withholding taxes and preparing W-2s, or by high-priced lawyers and accountants advising clients on tax matters, or by the government employees on the other side of the Internal Revenue desk.

As I struggled with my own income-tax return, visions kept going through my head of all the useful things that this hypothetical army could accomplish—the rows on rows of new houses, schools, churches, factories, autos, that they might be producing instead of rows on rows of numbers and of uneasy consciences.[1]

More recently, "The Treasury Department estimated that the public spent 613 million hours in 1977 filling out some 260 different tax forms." [2] That is roughly double the estimate we made in 1970— or more than 300,000 people working forty hours a week for fifty weeks a year. Yet even that is clearly a gross understatement.

A different kind of hidden cost arises when government acts through regulation. By means of regulation, legislators can spend our money without *either* the expenditure *or* the tax appearing in the government ledgers. For example, government regulations requiring antipollution equipment for automobiles impose a hidden tax of several hundred dollars on each purchaser of an automobile and a hidden expenditure by the government of that sum on the antipollution equipment. The significant difference from an open tax plus direct government expenditure is that neither the legislator nor the voter nor the automobile owner evaluates the expenditure properly—or even knows how large it is. Such antipollution requirements may or may not be desirable; they may or may not be worth their cost. Whether desirable or not, their cost is part of the total cost that we impose on ourselves through government.

Costs of this kind are so numerous and widespread, so interwoven with other costs, that there exists no satisfactory estimate of how much they amount to. What is clear is that they are substantial.

We propose in this chapter to present the background facts on how government spending grew to its present size, what the taxpayers' money is spent on, how it is raised and what the outstanding governmental obligations amount to, and finally, what has occurred in all these areas since President Reagan was inaugurated. We shall then, in the next chapter, turn to an analysis of why we have reached our present unsatisfactory situation and what we can do about it.

HOW GOVERNMENT SPENDING GREW

At the turn of the twentieth century, total spending by government amounted to less than 10 percent of the national income (Table 2.1). Equally important, two thirds of that total was spent by state and local governments. The largest item of expenditure was education, fol-

TABLE 2.1: **Government Spending as a Percentage of National Income in Selected Years**

Year	Federal	State and Local	Total
1902	3.2	6.1	9.3
1913	3.0	7.0	10.0
1922	6.3	9.2	15.5
1930	3.7	11.3	15.0
1940	12.5	10.8	23.3
1950	17.2	8.5	25.7
1960	22.4	10.4	32.8
1970	25.2	13.5	38.7
1980	28.4	12.7	41.1

lowed closely by highway construction and maintenance. More than half of all state and local expenditures was on education, highways, and local police, fire, and sanitation.

Only about 3 percent of national income, one third of total government spending, was spent by the federal government—and more than half of that was for defense and veterans benefits. Expenditures on the items that bulk so large in today's federal budget—"health, education, and welfare," as the most expensive department in the current U.S. government used to be named—amounted to only $10 million out of a total federal budget of less than $600 million. That was less than 2 percent of the federal budget and only six one-hundredths of 1 percent of the national income—2 percent of 3 percent. Today, federal expenditures on health, education, and welfare total more than 14 percent of national income, or *233 times as much as in 1902.*

Moreover, total federal government spending as a share of the national income was not very different in 1900 from what it had been throughout the previous century, or what it continued to be over the next three decades until the Great Depression, except only that it increased sharply with each major war—the War of 1812, the Civil

War, and World War I. Each time, as peace returned, federal spending tended to drift back to roughly 3 percent of national income.

For close to 150 years, spending by Washington showed no tendency to rise as a fraction of national income except when it was performing what was regarded as its major function—defending the nation. Its share stayed about 3 percent while the population of the United States swelled from 5 million persons hugging a narrow strip along the Atlantic coast to 125 million spread across a vast continent, while the United States changed from an overwhelmingly agricultural to a predominantly industrial country and became the driving force of the industrial revolution that transformed the world in the nineteenth and twentieth centuries, while the United States moved from a minor country of only peripheral interest to the Great Powers, to the Greatest Power of them all. *This remarkable fact should destroy once and for all the contention that economic growth and development require big government and especially centralized government.* It is a fact that should be taken to heart by the international planners of all those countries of the world that are euphemistically designated "the developing countries" but which for the most part are not developing but rather regressing under the iron hand of strong centralized governments.

During the early twentieth century, government spending did grow as a share of income, but entirely at the state and local level. As Table 2.1 and Figure 2.1 show, the state and local share rose fairly steadily from 1902—the first date for which we have comprehensive estimates—to 1930, nearly doubling by that year. At the same time, the federal share first went up, during and after World War I, and then declined. As a result, by 1930, state and local spending amounted to more than three times federal spending. Education and highways remained the largest items, and indeed, rose as a fraction of the total, accounting between them for well over half of total state and local spending.

The general picture is clear. Until the 1930s, the United States remained largely as its founders had envisaged it, a decentralized society in which the state and local governments were the primary govern-

FIGURE 2.1: **Federal, State and Local, and Total Government Spending as Percentage of National Income, for Selected Years, 1902–1980**

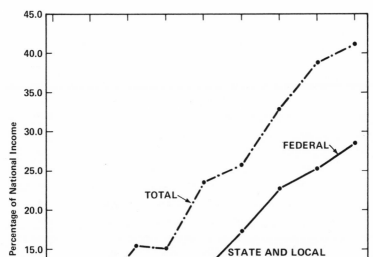

mental entities, with the federal government serving to defend the nation, administer a common commercial policy for the several states, adjudicate disputes arising among them, and provide a common framework of law—as an umpire and defender, not as a participant in the day-to-day lives of its citizens.

On the state and local level, as income and wealth increased, the citizens were willing to spend a larger fraction of their income on the services that they had decided to acquire through government, in particular education and highways. In addition, the shift of power from local communities to the states tended to increase total state and local spending for the same reasons—though on a smaller scale—as the subsequent shift of power from states to the federal government tended to increase total spending. (These reasons are spelled out in the next chapter.)

Competition disciplined the provision of these services as it did the provision of services produced through private markets, though less promptly and less effectively. Freedom to move meant that people who were dissatisfied with the services provided by their local or state government could vote not only at the ballot box but also with their feet—though voting with their feet was less effective at the state than at the local level.

The situation changed drastically after the Great Depression, as Figure 2.1 makes very clear. Funds raised and spent by state and local governments went down and then back up, but federal spending zoomed—from 3 percent of the national income to 30 percent, raising total government spending from 15 percent to more than 40 percent. Spending financed by the federal government rose from one third of spending financed by state and local governments to more than double such state and local spending.

In the *Federalist Papers*, James Madison went out of his way to reassure citizens who were fearful that the federal government would come to dominate the states. He pointed out that, "The number of individuals employed under the Constitution will be much smaller than the number employed under the particular States. There will consequently . . . be less of a personal influence on the side of the former than of the latter."[3] This prediction about the relative number of employees has been remarkably accurate. It remains true today. There are still many more direct employees of state and local government than of the federal government. In 1981, the federal government employed about 3 million civilians and about 1.5 million military personnel. State and local governments had over 13 million employees.

However, the framers of our Constitution did not envisage two recent developments: first, the invention of federal grants-in-aid to state and local governments, so that the funds to pay the salaries of many persons in state and local governments come from Washington; second, the enormous expansion of federal transfer payments to individuals who are not classified as employees. These developments have meant that the number of persons who directly or indirectly depend on spending financed by the federal government for their livelihood vastly exceeds the number who depend on spending financed by state and local governments.

Figure 2.1 conceals one important detail. During World War II, federal spending soared, reaching a peak of nearly half the national income at the height of the war in 1944. It then declined sharply as it had after earlier wars. The difference from earlier episodes is that, instead of declining to its prewar level, federal spending resumed the rapid rise that the New Deal had set in train.

This brief survey makes clear that the current problem of excessive government spending is primarily at the federal level. Indeed, many problems faced by states and localities derive from programs mandated by the federal government. Accordingly we turn to a more detailed examination of spending at the federal level, with special attention to what our money is being spent on.

FEDERAL GOVERNMENT SPENDING

Trying to find out what our money is spent on is easier promised than done. The 1984 budget documents submitted by the President in January 1983, for example, consist of four items: *The United States Budget in Brief, Fiscal Year 1984*, a summary of eighty-six pages intended for wide circulation; *The Budget of the United States Government, Fiscal Year 1984*, a hefty volume of 615 pages which contains "the Budget Message of the President and presents an overview of the President's budget proposals"; *Budget of the United States Government, 1984—Appendix*, an even more massive volume of 1,025 extra large pages which contains "detailed information on the various appropriations and funds that comprise the budget"; and finally *Special Analyses, Budget of the United States Government, 1984*, one volume of 363 pages containing "analyses that are designed to highlight specified program areas or provide other significant presentations of Federal budget data"—a grand total of 2,089 pages.

The several volumes are for sale to the public by the Government Printing Office at prices of $5.00, $7.50, $15.00, and $6.50 respectively—a total package price of $34.00. And that, no doubt, is a subsidized price financed out of the Government Printing Office's 1983 budget appropriation of over $120 million.

It is a major detective job to ferret out from these massive volumes how much the government spends on a particular program or category of programs. It is easy enough to find out that the Government Printing Office spent $91,237,000 in fiscal year 1982 (i.e., the twelve months ending September 30, 1982)—that is to be found in part 8, page 12, of the general budget document. It would be far more difficult to find out how much it cost to print the various budget documents just referred to. No doubt, a week's research in Washington could yield an estimate, but it would be imprecise. How much of the overhead, of the cost of equipment, etc., should be attributed to that one project? And how about figures for earlier years? And for a *calendar* year, rather than fiscal year?

How much it cost to print the budget documents is of no great importance, but it illustrates the extent to which the federal government has grown into an organization that is wholly beyond the comprehension of any single individual, literally uncontrollable by the collection of individuals whom we elect to Congress and to the presidency, feeding on itself—and us—and getting larger and larger like some enormous tumor.

Deliberate obfuscation renders the situation even more incomprehensible. Every program enacted to benefit a specific interest, even if the program is a price knowingly paid for gaining political support and campaign funds, is described as promoting the general welfare. Worse, if at all possible, the cost is buried in a total in order to disguise a sop to a special interest. Consider one particularly transparent case. "Conservation of agricultural resources" seems an appropriate object for governmental concern—until you realize that it is a euphemism for a program to subsidize farmers to keep land out of cultivation in order to keep up the price of farm products and the income of farmers. Or, take another example: the 1984 budget includes a proposed appropriation of $50 million to help finance the Summer Olympics. Where do you suppose that item is included? In the Department of Defense budget, under Operation and Maintenance, where another item is the more than $1,500 million budgeted for "Wildlife Conservation, Military Reservations."

Under the circumstances, we are forced to rely on the excellent summaries prepared by the Bureau of Economic Analysis of the Department of Commerce—financed out of the $50 million spent in (fiscal) 1982 by that department on "Economic and Statistical Analyses." In preparing the summaries, the Bureau of Economic Analysis drew on the data generated by the Bureau of the Census ($156 million) and the statistical divisions of the Department of Agriculture ($54 million) and the Department of Labor ($110 million), plus data generated by a score of other agencies, the expenditures of some of which, like the Federal Reserve System, are not recorded in any form in the mammoth budget volumes. As economic statisticians, we are delighted to have this plethora of data. As taxpayers, we are appalled at the cost.

Table 2.2 classifies total federal spending in three broad categories: (a) defense plus veterans benefits; (b) income support, Social Security, and welfare; and (c) all other. In view of what we have already said, we need hardly note that we offer no guarantees that the labels accurately describe the contents. To achieve comparability over time, we have expressed spending as a percentage of national income. The table gives estimates for each tenth year from 1930 to 1980. Figure 2.2 presents these decennial figures plus annual data from 1952 on. We start the annual data with 1952 because these are available in a convenient form only for that period. For earlier years, the estimates were built up by us from a number of bits and pieces.

In 1930, before the major shift in the role of government embodied in the New Deal, total federal spending amounted to less than 4 percent of the national income, and nearly two thirds of that

TABLE 2.2: **Federal Government Spending on Defense, Income Support, and Other as Percentage of National Income, for Selected Years, 1930–1980**

Year	Defense plus Veterans' Benefits	Income Support, Social Security, and Welfare	Other	Total
1930 ·	2.4	0.2	1.2	3.8
1940	3.6	1.6	7.3	12.5
1950	9.9	2.2	5.1	17.2
1960	12.1	4.8	5.5	22.4
1970	10.3	7.9	7.0	25.2
1980	7.3	12.6	8.5	28.4

went to defend the nation or to compensate the veterans of earlier wars. Of the rest, only a trivial amount—about 7 percent of the federal budget or one quarter of 1 percent of the national income—was in the category that by 1980 accounted for more than 40 percent of the budget and nearly one eighth of the national income: income support, Social Security, and welfare. The 1.2 percent of the national income spent in 1930 on "other" paid for interest on the federal debt, for the cost of running the executive, legislative, and judiciary branches of the government, for agricultural research and extensions, for maintaining airfields, and other activities.

By 1940, total spending had soared to one-eighth of the national income. With World War II under way in Europe, defense spending had understandably risen by 50 percent as a fraction of income. The increase in defense spending, large though it was, was moderate compared to the increase in the other categories, both of which multiplied more than sixfold. "Income support" ballooned as the recently enacted Social Security program began paying out benefits to retired persons and the "emergency" relief legislation produced substantial grants-in-aid to the states. "Other" expenditures ballooned as a wide range of New Deal programs gathered steam—agricultural price supports, public housing, Tennessee Valley Authority, National Labor

FIGURE 2.2: Federal Spending as Percentage of National Income

Percent of National Income

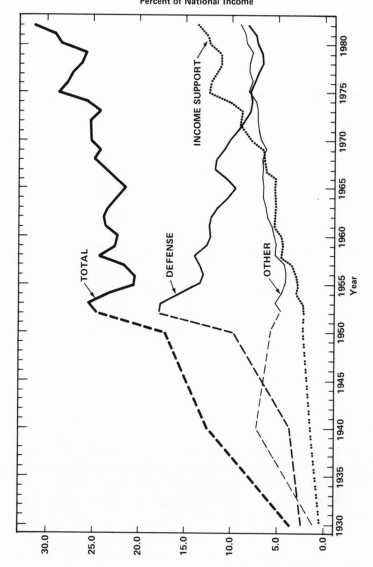

Relations Board, Securities and Exchange Commission, and on and on.

The post-World War II pattern is clear: total spending rose and fell, but the increases and decreases took place within a generally rising trend which more than doubled total spending as a percentage of the national income between 1940 and 1980. The ups and downs within this rising trend were accounted for partly by the ups and downs in military spending during first the Korean War and then the Vietnam War, and partly by the ups and downs in income support in response to successive cyclical recessions and expansions—each recession producing a sharp up, each expansion a partial retreat.

Military spending throughout was on a higher level than before World War II in response to the changed status of the United States in the world. But the trend was clearly and fairly sharply down— from a peak of nearly 18 percent in 1952, during the Korean War, to around 7 percent in the late 1970s, with only a mild rise since. All other categories, on the other hand, rose throughout the period, income support even more explosively than other. By 1970, income support was larger than other and by 1972 than defense. By 1976, other too was larger than defense.

Two things are clear from Table 2.2 and Figure 2.2: first, our budgetary problems have *not* been caused by runaway defense spending; second, the major culprit has been the explosive growth in income support, Social Security, and welfare, which went from around 2 percent of the national income in 1950 to more than 13 percent in 1982. Of the three components of this total, Social Security is the chief culprit. It accounted for less than 1 percent of the national income in 1952. Thirty years later, its share had multiplied tenfold, and it accounted for more than 8 percent of national income and two thirds of total expenditures in this category.

An even more striking indication of the explosion of the welfare state is what has happened to the number of persons receiving transfer payments from the federal government. In 1950, more than 10 million persons already received such payments. By 1980, that number was well over 50 million. Although per capita income nearly doubled from 1950 to 1980 (after allowing for inflation), more persons received payments in 1980 under the Aid to Families with Dependent Children program alone than received payments in 1950 under all the programs then in existence.

The growth in other seems moderate only by comparison with the growth in income support. It went from 5 percent of the national income in 1950 to twice that by 1982. Interest payments tripled, from 2 percent of the national income in 1950 to 6 percent in 1982. But some individual items—especially those encompassed by the Johnson Great Society programs—grew even more spectacularly. For example, expenditures on higher education went from $1 million (yes, million, *not* billion) in 1952 to $300 million in 1962 to nearly $9 billion in 1981, almost all of it in the form of aid (i.e., subsidies) to students.

Agriculture is another example. The number of persons employed on farms (including self-employed) declined from 6 million in 1952 to fewer than 3 million in 1982, yet total federal expenditures on agriculture rose from $1.25 billion in 1952 to close to $16 billion in 1982—from $210 per person employed on farms to over $6,000 per person. Apparently, the fewer the number of farmers, the greater their political clout. Both in 1952 and in 1982, most of the money went to support the price of farm crops: we paid farmers to keep output down; we bought some of the output and put it in storage; we subsidized the export of farm products. The intended result was to raise the price of farm products—that is, to make us pay more at the grocery counter for our food—and thereby transfer still more money from taxpayers to farmers. Nineteen eighty-three is scheduled to be another record year, with expenditures expected to zoom to more than $25 billion.

During the sixties and early seventies, the decline in spending on defense counterbalanced much of the increase in other spending. Nonetheless, total spending continued to rise. When the decline in defense spending tapered off and after 1979 was replaced by a rise, the full force of the increase in other categories of spending was reflected in total spending. As a result, from about 1973 or 1974 onward, total spending—if you average out peaks and troughs—rose without checks, and it precipitated the current budget crisis.

To summarize: the growth in total government spending from 15 percent of the national income in 1930 to over 45 percent today, and in spending by the federal government from less than 4 percent of the national income in 1930 to over 30 percent today, occurred only in small part because national defense (including veterans benefits) became more expensive. Defense accounted for less than 6 percentage points of the 26 percentage-point increase in the federal government's share of national income. Where did the rest of the money go? It went to finance *new* functions the government undertook. It went to transfer income from persons currently in the labor force to those who are retired, from persons who are employed to the unemployed. It went to pay for medical costs and costs of education that never before were a federal responsibility. It went to guide and direct our lives in a myriad of other ways.

States and localities have little choice about how to finance their spending. Most are required by their constitutions to balance their budgets. Even those that are not required to balance their budgets lack one alternative open to the federal government—creating money out of worthless paper or by accounting entries. States and cities must borrow on the open market, and that market imposes its own stringent discipline. But state and local governments do have a source of funds not available to the federal government, which is to say the federal government itself. During the past thirty years federal grants-in-aid to states grew from 12 percent of total state spending in 1950 to 21 percent in 1980. Because of their own constitutional and practical restraints, and aided by grants from Uncle Sam, state and local governments have run surpluses rather more frequently than deficits. During the 1970s, indeed, they recorded a surplus every year—again with the indirect help of the federal government. Inflation generated by the federal government tended to raise state revenues faster than state expenses, especially in states that had graduated income taxes. Bracket creep was just as effective in raising state taxes without legislation as it was in raising federal taxes. The growth of deficits as of government spending is a problem that must be attacked primarily at the federal level.

DEFICITS

The daily or weekly news media and the TV nightly news give the false impression that the major problems with the federal budget are, first, the size of the deficit and, second, the mounting public debt. It's not so. It would be hard to be further from the truth, as Table 2.3 makes clear. Taxes and spending are the real culprits, not deficits and debt.

Tax receipts have risen on average only slightly less rapidly than spending. Between 1950 and 1970, some years had a surplus, some a deficit. The net deficit averaged only about one tenth of 1 percent of the national income per year. From 1970 on, the situation changed. Every year has seen a deficit. The deficits for the thirteen years from 1970 to 1982 averaged 2.5 percent of the national income. Even so, the deficit has not shown a consistent tendency to increase; it has gone up and down. It was 2.5 percent in 1971 and 2.6 percent in 1981; it was 5.6 percent in 1975 and 6.1 percent in 1982. The real problem is not the bookkeeping deficit; it is the consistent growth in both spending and taxes. *The federal budget would have been roughly balanced, or gained a surplus in 1980, 1981, and 1982, had total spending been held down to the same percentage of the national income as in 1979.*

Like the concern with the deficit, the wailing and gnashing of teeth over the supposedly trillion-dollar public debt is a false emotion. In the first place, the figures cited for the public debt owned by private citizens are almost invariably overstated because they include the debt owned by the Federal Reserve System—$130 billion at the end of 1982. But the Federal Reserve is "public" only through misleading packaging and labeling. In every relevant respect, the Fed is part of the government. In the second place, while the dollar total of the debt has quadrupled since the end of World War II—from around

TABLE 2.3: **Federal Spending, Tax Receipts, Deficit, and Outstanding Debt as Percentage of National Income, for Selected Years, 1930–1980**

Year	Spending	Tax Receipts	Deficit	Outstanding Debt
1930	3.7	4.1	−0.4	21.1
1940	12.5	10.8	1.7	45.4
1950	17.2	21.1	−3.9	84.1
1960	22.4	23.1	−0.7	50.5
1970	25.2	23.7	1.5	26.8
1980	28.4	25.5	2.9	27.8

$200 billion then to $800 billion at the end of 1982—prices have more than quadrupled, *so the debt adjusted for inflation has actually fallen.* Moreover, our economy has grown, so, as Table 2.3 shows, the debt has fallen even more sharply when it is expressed as a percentage of national income. Just after World War II, the national debt amounted to roughly one year's national income. By 1980, it had fallen to a little over a quarter of a year's national income.

What explains this paradox? Deficits occur year after year, yet debt declines both in real terms and as a fraction of national income. The answer is clear. By paying the debt off in cheaper and cheaper dollars, we have in fact defaulted on much of it. Or, to use polite language, we have imposed a hidden tax on many holders of the public debt—particularly those who were persuaded to *buy* the debt, particularly savings bonds, by eloquent appeals to their patriotism. The deficit recorded on the books is highly misleading. It should be reduced by the inflation tax imposed on each person who patriotically purchased government bonds.

But that is cold comfort. We have a debt problem many times more serious that is not recorded on the books. The debt that is recorded on the books is only the tip of the iceberg. We are committed to pay future benefits to retired persons under Social Security, federal employee and railroad retirement programs, and future medical costs under Medicare. Future receipts from the taxes now on the books to meet these costs are far from adequate. TV trumpeted the news that the presidential commission had "saved Social Security." But the system was not saved. Band-Aids may hide the bleeding, but they don't cure the wound. Estimates of the unfunded debt vary, yet even the most conservative one sets it at currently more than $6 trillion—yes, trillion, not billion—and more pessimistic estimates go as high as $10 trillion, which is more than seven times as large as the official public debt.

THE RECORD SINCE 1980

With this background, it is time to zero in on what has happened since Ronald Reagan was elected President. The data in Table 2.4 are comparable to those given in earlier tables. However, the "year" in Table 2.4 is the government's fiscal year ending September 30, instead of the calendar year ending December 31, as in the earlier tables. Here we use the fiscal year to enable us to make better use of the figures in the government's budget documents, all of which are on a fiscal year basis.

Ronald Reagan was elected President in 1980, but he did not assume office until January 1981, by which time four months of the 1981 fiscal year had already passed and the pipeline was pretty well full for the rest of that fiscal year. So, the first fiscal year on which he could have any significant impact was 1982, beginning in October 1981.

At first glance, the impression is one of business pretty much as usual: total spending continued its sharp climb, because of rises in income support and defense. The only apparent changes are these: first, the other category stabilized from 1982 to 1983; and, second, receipts fell from 1981 to 1983. Both changes are partly attributable to Reagan's policies. He persuaded Congress in 1981 to cut some categories of spending—or, rather, to cut the increases in some categories of spending. He also persuaded Congress to cut tax rates in that same year. True, for 1981 and 1982, those tax cuts were largely

TABLE 2.4: **Federal Government Expenditures on Defense, Income Support, and Other; Total Expenditures; Receipts; and Deficit as Percentage of National Income, fiscal years 1980–83**

Year (ending Sept.)	Defense plus Veterans' Benefits	Income Support, Social Security, and Welfare	Other	Total	Total Receipts	Deficit
		Expenditures on				
1980	7.6	12.0	8.2	27.8	25.3	2.5
1981	8.0	12.7	8.3	29.0	26.7	2.3
1982	8.7	13.4	8.5	30.6	25.6	5.0
1983 (*est.*)	9.2	13.9	8.5	31.6	24.5	7.1

offset by increases in Social Security taxes that had been legislated earlier, as well as by bracket creep. However, if the tax-rate cuts had not occurred, the higher Social Security taxes and bracket creep would not have been offset at all.

As it was, the main reason why receipts declined as a fraction of income in 1982 and 1983, rather than remaining stable, was *not* the Reagan tax program. Rather, it was the effect of the long and severe recession from mid-1981 up to the very end of 1982. That recession, too, was responsible for some part of the increase in spending, particularly through benefits paid to the unemployed.

Four categories of spending increased consistently and markedly from 1980 to 1983. Look at Table 2.5.

Spending on defense increased the most—carrying out President Reagan's campaign commitment to strengthen the national defense.

The second largest increase was in a class of programs that together can accurately be described as middle-class or, indeed, upper-class welfare: Social Security and other government administered retirement and disability programs, plus Medicare.

The long and sharp recession increased both unemployment compensation and subsidies to agriculture. This third category accounted for between a quarter and a third of the total net increase.

The fourth item showing a large increase was net interest, an

TABLE 2.5: **Change in Expenditures on Budget Items as Percentage of National Income, 1980–1983, 1981–1983**

	Change in Percentage of National Income	
Items	1980–1983	1981–1983
Major Increases		
Defense plus Veterans Benefits	+ 1.61	+ 1.24
Middle-Class Welfare (retirement, disability, Medicare)	+ 1.44	+ 0.90
Recession-induced (unemployment insurance and agricultural subsidies)	+ 1.02	+ 0.95
Net Interest	+ 0.88	+ 0.42
Total of Major Increases	+ 4.95	+ 3.51
Major Decreases		
Natural Resources, Energy, Transportation, Community and Regional Development	− 0.63	− 0.49
Education, Training, and Employment	− 0.44	− 0.38
Revenue Sharing	− 0.17	− 0.06
Total of Major Decreases	− 1.24	− 0.93
All Other	+ 0.04	+ 0.02
Total Net Change	+ 3.75	+ 2.60

item that is grossly overstated because it does not allow for the simultaneous effect of inflation in reducing the public debt as a fraction of income.

Together, these four categories rose nearly one-third more than the total net increase in expenditures.

The offsetting reductions are spread throughout the budget. The largest reduction is in a category of programs that can perhaps be described as expenditures on things: spending on natural resources, energy, transportation, community and regional development. A second category showing a net reduction consists of a variety of programs directed at elementary, secondary, vocational, and higher education, and at job training and direct employment. These are hard to characterize simply. Most are directed at benefiting relatively low-income persons—notably the training and employment programs, and education programs for the disadvantaged and handicapped, which together account for more than half of total spending in this category. But they also include expenditures on higher education, which mostly affect middle- or upper-income persons. A major reduction was the elimination of the CETA program, which was castigated widely as a boondoggle.

A third category showing a reduction consists of grants of funds by the federal government to state and local governments not for specific programs but for use as the recipient government units see fit.

A fascinating aspect of this list of reductions is that it does not include any of the welfare programs for the poor—it does *not* include Aid to Families with Dependent Children, *not* SSI (Supplementary Security Income), *not* food stamps, *not* housing subsidies, *not* Medicaid, *not* social services. Some of these items went down, some went up, but both the increases and decreases were slight. Taken as a whole, the best description is that *welfare programs for the poor were held constant as a fraction of income.*

These facts paint a very different picture from that drawn by either President Reagan's supporters or his opponents. Welfare for the poor has not been cut. To that extent, the charge that President Reagan has destroyed the safety net for the poor is not correct. Welfare for the middle class and upper-income class went up sharply. To that extent, the charge that changes in spending were biased against the poor is correct. However, the blame, or credit, for this development can hardly be assigned to President Reagan. He proposed in 1981 and again in 1982 major changes in the Social Security programs that were designed to hold down their cost. Not surprisingly, these changes, which would have introduced greater evenhandedness, were denounced and ridiculed by the very legislators who complained loudest about the supposed "unfairness" of the President's proposed cuts in the budget.

The only substantial decreases in spending were in programs largely administered by states and localities, whether federal programs in education, training and employment, transportation, community and regional development, or state programs financed by revenue sharing. These programs are so diverse that it is literally impossible to judge how cuts in them affected different income classes. Partly these reductions reflect the President's commitment to federalization—to returning powers and responsibility to the states and to local communities. Mostly, the cuts came here because both the President and the Congress were under pressure to hold down spending, and state and local governments offered less resistance to cuts than other pressure groups. Expediency, not principle, ruled.

On the side of taxes, President Reagan's opponents attacked his proposed cuts as favoring the rich. Here again the situation is more complex. The increase in Social Security taxes did raise the taxes imposed on lower-income groups—but those increases were legislated during Carter's term, not Reagan's. Bracket creep because of inflation does affect low-income and middle-income groups—but again, inflation was an inheritance from the Carter years, and it has come down sharply since the 1980 election. The first two installments of the across-the-board cuts in tax rates—those that took effect in 1981 and 1982—roughly offset bracket creep. The final installment, which took effect on July 1, 1983, more than offset bracket creep. Thus, it is the first *real* cut in tax rates. Further, the provision for indexing the tax rates for inflation assures that bracket creep will not rear its ugly head in the future. These changes were evenhanded or, if anything, biased toward low-income and middle-income groups, not toward the rich. The one tax change that can be said to favor the rich was the reduction in the top rate on "unearned" income from 70 to 50 percent, which took effect in 1981. But that change was not recommended by President Reagan. It was added in the course of the legislative process in the House of Representatives by the Democrat-controlled Committee on Ways and Means. Moreover, it has produced higher not lower revenue.

The Reagan years have seen a start toward achieving President Reagan's objective of cutting tax rates. They have seen no progress toward his parallel objectives of cutting government spending and balancing the budget. Even after the fullest possible allowance for the effect of the recession on government spending and the deficit, both spending and the deficit have continued to rise as a fraction of income. Progress on these objectives will have to wait for President Reagan's second term.

3

CAUSES AND CURE: GOVERNMENT SPENDING, TAXES, AND DEFICITS

*I place economy among the first and most important virtues, and public debt as the greatest of dangers to be feared.
. . . To preserve our independence, we must not let our rulers load us with public debt . . . we must make our choice between economy and liberty or confusion and servitude. . . .*

If we run into such debts, we must be taxed in our meat and drink, in our necessities and comforts, in our labor and in our amusements. . . . If we can prevent the government from wasting the labor of the people, under the pretense of caring for them, they will be happy.

—Thomas Jefferson[1]

WE HAVE DOCUMENTED the drastic increase over the past fifty years in the role of government, especially the federal government. This chapter examines the causes for that increase and suggests ways that the trend can be reversed.

Special interest or single-issue politics are a frequent explanation for the growth in government. A government program, particularly at the federal level, almost always confers substantial benefits on a relatively small group while at the same time spreading the costs widely (and hence thinly) over the population at large. As a result, the few have a strong incentive to lobby intensively for the program. The many don't bother even to inform themselves about it, let alone to devote money and effort to opposing it. A legislator who believes that the program on net harms the public is caught in an impossible position. A vote against such a program generates concentrated opposition from the few who will benefit from it, but at best only weak and diffused support from the many who will pay for it.

As Congressman Philip Gramm put it:

[E]very time you vote on every issue, all the people who want the program are looking over your right shoulder and nobody's looking over your left shoulder. They're sending letters back home telling people whether Phil Gramm cares about the old, the poor, the sick, the bicycle riders . . . the list goes on. It's perfectly legitimate. The problem is that nobody's looking over the left shoulder. . . .

So in being fiscally responsible under such circumstances, we're asking more of people than the Lord asks. At least I know if I do good—if I take the Bible literally—when I get to Heaven, it's going to be written in the Golden Book. I know here it will never be known. [2]

Although correct, this explanation does not go far enough. After all, the same incentive for special interest groups to pressure legislators existed before 1933 as well as after 1933, yet the growth of government before 1933 was slight but after 1933 explosive. As the preceding chapter demonstrates, the catalyst for the explosive growth of spending was the transfer of power from state and local governments to the federal government. That, too, could have occurred before 1933, yet did not. Why not?

WHY GOVERNMENT SPENDING
EXPLODED IN THE 1930s

The major reason these changes took place when they did was the basic shift that occurred in public opinion. In *Free to Choose* we said, it shifted "from belief in individual responsibility, laissez-faire, and a decentralized and limited government to belief in social responsibility and a centralized and powerful government . . . to protect individuals from the vicissitudes of fortune and to control the operation of the economy in the 'general interest' " (p. 92).

After all, this is a democracy. If the people disapprove of what their government is doing, they can change that government at election time—every two years when they elect all congressmen and one third of the senators, and every four years when they elect the President. The change in public opinion in 1933 brought changes in the people whom the electorate sent to Washington. During the sixty-four years from the first presidential election after the Civil War to 1933, the Republicans controlled the White House for forty-eight years, the Senate for fifty-two years, and the House for forty-four years. Beginning in 1933, the tables were turned. During the forty-eight years from 1933 to 1981, the Democrats controlled the White House for thirty-two years, the Senate for forty-four years, and the House for forty-four years. This turnaround was a dramatic result of the fundamental change that had occurred in what the public wanted. Moreover, the long continuance of the same pattern after 1933 demonstrates that for many years thereafter the public at large was satisfied with what it got.

A similar change in public opinion was already manifest in Western Europe long before 1933. A number of countries enacted extensive programs directed at providing security from cradle to grave—unemployment benefits, old-age benefits, socialized medicine, child support, and so on. In some countries, the change went further and led to a growing nationalization of industries as well. Before 1933, such a change in policy was not a part of public discussion in the

United States. It was a subject for discussion among intellectuals on the campus and, to a lesser extent, among some journalists.

The Great Depression brought unemployment, bread lines, and business failures. It caused a loss in faith in the prevailing economic system, which in turn led the public at large to join the intellectuals in assigning a larger role to government. The New Deal was the result. For Uncle Sam to take upon his shoulders all the cares and responsibilities of his people sounded like a splendid idea. Faith in that idea remained strong for decades. But after half a century, the faith weakened as government grew and the costs to the citizen mounted—not alone in money, even more in the loss of freedom.

A big and centralized government is an unavoidable result of a government that seeks to perform the wide range of functions that the public has assigned to it in recent decades. Only a centralized government could be expected to act effectively to maintain full employment, prevent recessions, and avoid inflation. No state or local government can handle such problems, which are national in scope. Only a big government could conceivably protect over 200 million individual citizens against the hazards of old age, illness, and unemployment, to say nothing of floods and all other vicissitudes of fortune. It takes an army of social workers, administrators, statisticians— you name them—to run a government that seeks to deal with the specific problems of specific individuals or groups.

The truth is that not even a big and centralized government can successfully perform these functions. This fact has been demonstrated over and over again—in the most extreme form, in the communist countries of Russia and China, where Marxist doctrine holds that citizens proceed on the principle "from each according to his ability, to each according to his need." In those societies the principle never worked; instead, government officials became "the new class" of privileged autocrats, enslaving the masses. In our own country, one social welfare program after another has turned out to have effects opposite to those that were intended by the well-meaning people who supported them. Good intentions alone are not enough. Governmental employees, no less than employees of private businesses, will put their own interests above the interests of others. Calling them public servants does not alter that fact.

✗ In the immediate aftermath of the Great Depression, the New Deal seemed to produce desirable results. When certain programs failed to achieve the intended result, it became popular to say that they failed for lack of sufficient funding. This logic was astonishing! Each disappointment tended to lead to expanding the particular social program and increased the amount of money devoted to it. Total government spending grew and grew and grew.

Moreover, new programs typically start small, but many have the potential of becoming huge. For example, when Social Security was first introduced, few people qualified for benefits. As late as 1950, twenty-four workers paid Social Security taxes for every person who received benefits. Small taxes could provide substantial benefits and still yield a surplus. By 1980, there were only about three workers paying for each recipient of benefits, and the ratio is heading still lower, toward two workers for one beneficiary. Total costs go up and so do the taxes that have to be imposed on the workers to finance payments to the retired. In addition, the benefits have been increased almost year to year—certainly from election year to election year.

✰ Government spending thus acquires a momentum of its own from two sources: the tolerance of the public as it seeks to achieve its objectives by spending more money and the expansion of programs that start small.

WHY DEFICITS RATHER THAN HIGHER TAXES

✐ Higher government spending generates opposition from the public for two very different reasons. One is their disappointment with results. The other is their reaction against the burden of taxes.

The taxes required to pay for a particular program are small when spread thinly over the population as a whole. But small tax burdens mount up. True, many taxes are imposed in a hidden, indirect form, such as corporation taxes, excise taxes, or tariffs, and all these are included in the cost of products. In addition, the withholding of taxes from wages reduces the visibility of the personal income tax. Even so, individuals are keenly aware of paying sales taxes, personal income taxes, and property taxes. By the 1970s, a taxpayer revolt had emerged, fueled by the belief that we are not getting our money's worth for the taxes we are paying.

The taxpayer revolt was thrust into national prominence by the passage of Proposition 13 in California. It then spread much more widely, making it politically profitable to try to reduce taxes and certainly to avoid increasing them.

Despite these developments, the pressure for spending continues. Precisely because social welfare programs do not achieve their objectives, the evils that they were intended to repair stand out. In the private sphere, failure typically means *less* money to spend. In government, failure generates pressure for *more* money to spend. And a politically attractive way to yield to this pressure is to vote for more spending, but not to vote for more taxes.

The federal government can spend without either legislating taxes or borrowing because the federal government controls the money supply. It can finance spending by creating money. Moreover, the resulting inflation has the side effect of raising tax revenues by means of bracket creep, thereby increasing the burden of "old" taxes, those voted in the past. Some years ago, a member of the Senate Finance Committee commented that inflation had subjected persons of modest incomes to tax rates that it would have been impossible for Congress to legislate openly. When these rates *were* legislated, they were applied to levels of income received only by the well-to-do—and this made it politically possible to legislate them. No member of Congress has since that time had to vote to impose these rates on what are now modest incomes, and no President has ever had to sign such a bill. Inflation has done for Congress what Congress would not have been willing to do for itself.

Inflation and borrowing are forms of hidden taxation that do not arouse taxpayer resentment in the same way as the direct imposition of taxes. Moreover, they can be imposed without requiring any legislator to vote for them explicitly. Equally important, the culprits who produce inflation have many faces. Congress blames grasping unions or greedy manufacturers. More recently, Congress blames the Federal Reserve, and the Fed returns the compliment by blaming Congress and others, and so around and around the blame goes. No legislator has ever gone back to his constituents and been asked by one of them, "Why did you vote to make every dollar in my pocket or my bank account worth ninety cents?" Yet that is precisely what a 10 percent inflation does in the course of a year. It is the precise equivalent of a tax of 10 percent on every person's cash.

WHY IS IT SO HARD TO CHANGE?

If, as we believe, there has been a basic change in public opinion in recent years, why does that change seem to have had so little effect on the course of events? After all, the change in public opinion in 1933 was followed by the rapid growth of the New Deal. Within the first few years after President Roosevelt took office, major new institutions had been established and new measures adopted. By 1940, total federal spending was more than three times as large a fraction of national income as it had been in 1930, and nondefense spending was more than six times as large. Why, then, does the effect of the recent change in opinion reflected in the 1980 election appear to be so modest?

One reason is an optical illusion: hindsight foreshortens time. Many of the people who were in the front lines fighting to produce changes in the 1930s must have regarded events as moving extraordinarily slowly. No doubt they were impatient to achieve their objectives more rapidly, just as many of us are now impatient to achieve ours. In retrospect, the four years of President Roosevelt's first term seem shorter than the first two years of President Reagan's first term. Moreover, most big reforms introduced by President Roosevelt were adopted in the first three months after his election—his honeymoon period—just as President Reagan succeeded in achieving some big changes in a comparable period. Enough time has now passed for the New Deal changes to have had their full effect—but not enough time for the Reagan changes.

An optical illusion is only one reason. A more important reason, in our opinion, is the asymmetry between the resistance to increasing the size of government and to decreasing it, between introducing new programs and dismantling them. An increase in the size of government is far less likely to run into concentrated and effective resistance—and, indeed, sabotage—than a decrease in the size of government. True, the tyranny of the status quo operates for both. Known ways of doing things are preferred; change is resisted. However, the resistance is far less when the change benefits a few at the expense of many then when it involves taking away from a few in order to benefit many.

Under the best of circumstances, a massive government cannot be reordered and reduced overnight. A government that has been built up over decades cannot be dismantled in one or two years. The image that comes to mind is of a supertanker. The officer on the bridge must order a turn many miles before the actual turn occurs.

The undoubted difficulty of slowing the growth of government, let alone reducing the size of a massive government, manifests itself in what has come to be called the iron triangle. At one corner are the direct beneficiaries of a law; at a second, the legislative committees and their staffs; at a third, the bureaucracy administering a law. These three powerful tyrannies enforce the status quo.

TYRANNY OF BENEFICIARIES

The reactions of a group of persons who believe that they are benefiting from a government program—or, at any rate, believe that they would be harmed by its elimination—reminds us of what Jeremy Bentham wrote two centuries ago about moneylending. Said Bentham: "The business of a moneylender . . . has nowhere, nor at any time, been a popular one. Those who have the resolution to sacrifice the present to future, are natural objects of envy to those who have sacrificed the future to the present. The children who have eaten their cake are the natural enemies of the children who have theirs. While the money is hoped for, and for a short time after it has been received, he who lends it is a friend and benefactor: by the time the money is spent, and the evil hour of reckoning is come, the benefactor is found to have changed his nature, and to have put on the tyrant and the oppressor. It is an oppression for a man to reclaim his own money; it is none to keep it from him."[3]

There is one important difference. In Bentham's example, the person who received the money will have to pay it back. With a typical government program, the persons who initially receive the benefits from a program are typically *not* the persons who would currently be harmed by its elimination: one group benefits when the program is first instituted; a different group is hurt if and when it is terminated. Consider a tariff. When a tariff is first enacted, persons who produce the product covered by the tariff benefit. They have a sheltered market for their goods and can charge higher prices. The owners and workers in existing enterprises are all made better off. Subsequently, their prosperity will encourage others to produce the same product. As others enter the industry, returns are driven down roughly to the level where they were before. The result is that a larger number of persons are engaged in the industry, all earning roughly the same income that they had earned when employed earlier in other industries. When the tariff is eliminated, the owners will have to accept a lower price for the product they sell. As losses occur, some companies will abandon the industry. Soon, everybody will be back more or less where he was before. The gains went to the earliest persons in the industry; the losses were borne by those who came after.

Or, consider a simpler example. Mr. Smith uses savings of $60,000 accumulated over many years to build a factory producing widgets much desired by consumers. Mr. Jones uses savings of $60,000 accumulated over many years to buy a medallion entitling him to operate a taxicab in New York City, rendering services much desired by consumers. Both Smith and Jones have created private wealth— embodied in a factory in the one case, in a taxicab medallion in the other. Both use their private wealth to serve the public. From a private point of view, their cases are indistinguishable and equally deserving of commendation.

From the public point of view, the two cases are radically different. Smith's use of his private wealth adds to the total supply of physical capital available to serve the public; it adds to the productive capacity of the community. Jones's use of his private wealth does not. It simply transfers that wealth from Jones to the person who owned the medallion before. The taxicab medallion has a market value only because the number of medallions is artificially limited. Jones is a member of a governmentally created cartel. As a result, the price that customers must pay for the services rendered by the cab exceeds the cost of owning and running the cab and, of course, the value that Jones attributes to his own labor. In the absence of the cartel, the excess of returns over costs would lead more persons to enter the taxicab business. The fares fixed by local authorities for taxicab service would go down, or cabs would be more easily obtainable, until costs and returns came into balance. Consumers would be better off, as would the additional owners of cabs and all hired drivers of cabs. But Jones would be worse off: the medallion for which he paid $60,000 would be worthless.

We make this comparison not to attack the limitation of taxicab licenses (though that limitation deserves to be attacked), but to illuminate a major source of confusion about the role of government in regulating industry and a major source of the difficulty in ending undesirable regulation. To continue with our example, suppose that the numerical limitation on taxicabs were eliminated, and licenses were freely issued. The effect on Jones would be identical to the effect on Smith of government expropriation of his factory without compensation—something specifically prohibited by the Fifth Amendment to the Constitution ("Nor shall private property be taken for public use without just compensation"). It is entirely understandable that cab owner Jones would oppose that measure with the same righteous wrath with which factory owner Smith would oppose the expropriation of his property.

Although privately identical, the two actions would have wholly different effects on the public interest: the one, eliminating Jones's medallion, promotes the public interest by eliminating "artificial" wealth that was created by government edict and that harms the public; the other, expropriating Smith's factory, hurts the public interest by confiscating physical wealth that benefits the public. On an ethical level, Jones is as deserving of compensation for the taking of his wealth as Smith is for the taking of his wealth—the only qualification being that Jones acquired the medallion in the knowledge that an exclusive privilege granted by government *could be withdrawn by government.* Yet, if that ethic were really applied, it would be disastrous. If government were required to compensate every vested interest in society, however created, for any harm to it caused by legislation, the cost would be impossible to bear. Aside from the impossibility of determining even the monetary effects of legislation, the effect would be to enshrine the status quo and prevent the correction of past errors.

Our simple comparison has relevance to a wide range of problems—ICC restrictions on trucking and busing, CAB restrictions on airlines, FCC controls on television, radio, and telephones, price ceilings on crude oil and natural gas, licensing of occupations, rent controls, agricultural price supports, tariffs and import quotas, and on and on. All are cases of private wealth created by measures that harm the public. We have created a Frankenstein monster we cannot easily subdue. Under these circumstances, it is not hard to see why there is a tyranny of beneficiaries, why it is so much harder to dismantle a program than it is to put a new one in place.

TYRANNY OF POLITICIANS

Throughout recorded history whenever leaders have been chosen by some method of voting, the aspirants for leadership have bought votes. Traditionally they have bought votes either with their own money or with a patron's money. To some extent, they still do so. But something new has been added! Since the 1930s, the technique of buying votes with the voters' own money has been expanded to an extent undreamed of by earlier politicians.

In his marvelous biography of George Washington, James Flexner tells how Washington achieved his first political victory, election to the Virginia House of Burgesses in 1758 on his second try when he was twenty-six years old: "Such reports from his campaign manager as 'Will the hatter and his oily spouse show the greatest spirit in the cause,' were promising, and, indeed he got the votes of 309 of the 396 voters. A supporter attributed his victory to 'your humane and equitable treatment of each individual and your ardent zeal for the common cause.' Liquid persuasives were not overlooked by his friends, who distributed twenty-eight gallons of rum, fifty of rum punch, thirty-four of wine, forty-six of beer, and two of cider. Far from protesting the bill sent to him for this quart and a half per voter, Washington wrote, 'I hope no exception were taken to any that voted against me, but that all were alike treated and all had enough. . . . My only fear is that you spent with too sparing a hand.' "[4]

Today, candidates still spend their own money to buy votes, as well as the money of a much wider group of patrons—of which the PACs are the most recent. In addition, presidential candidates get direct government subsidies to finance their campaigns—thereby tapping directly the voters' own money. But that is only the tip of the iceberg. The major way in which candidates buy votes with the voters' own money is very different—by promising all voters goodies supposedly to be paid for by other voters. Candidates are voluble in boasting about the new spending programs that they will support. They are generally silent about who will pay the bill. If they say anything, they name someone other than the voters addressed: the "rich," or if the candidate is from California, the residents of New York; if he is from New York, the residents of California.

Patrons remain important: the lobbyists, the political action committees, the various other kinds of special interest groups that provide campaign funds for candidates. Surely, that is a major reason why our tax laws are so complex and so difficult to simplify. Members of Congress now get much support from groups that seek either to have special benefits introduced into the tax system, or else to prevent benefits from being withdrawn, or finally to prevent special impositions from being levied on them. How can it all be stopped?

Truly simplify the tax system, and all of a sudden a major source of patronage for politicians would disappear.

At the federal level, the tyranny of politicians merges with the tyranny of bureaucracy. The legislature has itself become an enormous bureaucracy. The 535 members of the House and Senate are served directly by nearly 20,000 employees, or forty-five staff members to one congressman. It now costs us close to $2.5 million for each senator, and close to $1 million for each representative—to pay their salaries, the salaries of their assistants, and the other costs they incur. And this does not include the cost of the many employees in other parts of the legislative branch, such as the Library of Congress, the Government Printing Office, and the General Accounting Office. Like every other bureaucracy, this one, too, has a life and inertia of its own.

TYRANNY OF BUREAUCRACY

The centralization and the enlargement of the functions of government inevitably require a change in the way that government operates. The 435 members of the House of Representatives and the one hundred senators cannot begin to be informed about all of the activities on which they now legislate. The President and the thirteen members of his Cabinet cannot begin to be informed on all the activities that they are supposed to administer. It would take far more than twenty-four hours a day for our legislators just to *read* all of the laws that they are required to vote on, let alone to investigate and evaluate them. They still pass the laws, but they do so primarily on the advice of, or under pressure from, their large staffs of assistants— or the ever more numerous lobbyists who besiege them.

Inevitably, the actual conduct of government is delegated to bureaucrats. The number of bureaucrats has grown immensely in the course of years. From 1933 to 1982, the population of the United States didn't quite double, but the total number of employees of the federal government alone multiplied almost fivefold. In addition, hundreds of thousands, perhaps millions, of persons who are not listed as civilian employees of the federal government are employed by the federal government as consultants, advisers on contract, and the like. The words of the Declaration of Independence express the reaction of many citizens to this development: "He [King George] has erected a Multitude of new Offices, and sent hither Swarms of Officers to harass our People, and eat out their Substance."

The terms "Multitude of New Offices" and "Swarms of Officers" describe vividly what has happened in the past four or five decades. But we now have no "he" to blame. *He* has not now done this. *We* have done it to ourselves. *We* have erected the "Multitude of new Offices" to achieve functions that "our People" believed could be performed by those "Swarms of Officers."

The fault is not in the character of the particular individuals who serve as bureaucrats. On the whole, they are a fair and representative sample of the citizenry. Many public servants are dedicated to pursuing the purposes for which they have been hired. Like some of the rest of us, some are lazy, incompetent, and inefficient. The problem is not people as individuals; the problem is the system.

By its very nature, a large bureaucracy tends to proceed by laws of its own. To call individuals public servants does not change their human characteristics. Each of us tends to put his or her interests first. Those interests will include some that are broad and unselfish—doing good or benefiting mankind—but even so, each of us will interpret doing good and benefiting mankind in terms of our own values. And what some regard as good others will regard as bad. Those interests will also include some that are less broad and more selfish—or some of us would say, less pretentious—improving our lot in life and the lot of our children.

The key characteristics of bureaucrats are these: first, they spend other people's money; second, they have a bottom line, a proof of success, that is very distant and difficult to define. Under those conditions, a major incentive for every bureaucrat is to become more powerful—and this is true whether the bureaucrat is dominated by broad and unselfish interests or by narrow and selfish interests. In either case, being more powerful will enable the bureaucrat to pursue those interests more effectively. In most cases, the way for a bureaucrat to become more powerful is to have more people under his or her control—to expand the scope of whatever piece of the gigantic governmental structure is that bureaucrat's domain.

Every large bureaucracy, government or private, knows that the way it conducts its affairs is the best way. This universal perception is effectively challenged in government only at a time of real crisis—in time of national disaster, or war—when something simply *must* be done differently. In business, the bottom line of profit provides an effective and continuous challenge. Businesses that are operated in accordance with the law of bureaucratic inertia fail. That is an advantage of the private market that is seldom recognized. Government bureaucrats may be just as perceptive as private entrepreneurs, just as wise, just as innovative in deciding what projects to undertake, but there is no mechanism for terminating unsuccessful experiments; instead, they tend to be expanded in order to bury small failures in a large venture which itself will one day fail. A private business that undertakes an unsuccessful experiment has no choice: it recognizes its mistake or goes bankrupt—unless it can get government to subsidize it. That is why the *loss* component of the profit and loss system is far more important than the *profit* component. Directors of companies can overlook smaller than expected profits for years, but losses make them vulnerable and anxious.

One of the authors was first impressed by the law of bureaucratic inertia during World War II, when, as a junior bureaucrat in the U.S. Treasury Department, he helped to devise the present withholding tax (something, incidentally, for which the other author has never forgiven him). We consulted German refugees who knew the German tax system. They described in detail their method of withholding at source and assured us that it was the only feasible way. We consulted British experts. They assured us that the very different method followed in Britain was the only feasible way. We decided that both were models of what to avoid, not imitate.

If today you were to ask a high Internal Revenue Service official whether income taxes could be effectively collected without a withholding system, he would consign you to the loony bin. But in 1942, when we were devising our system, *the IRS was the chief obstacle to its adoption*. IRS bureaucrats insisted that their way of collecting the income tax directly from the taxpayer after he finished a year's work was the only feasible way. We were starry-eyed theorists to suppose that withholding at source was administratively feasible.

One other enormously important feature of bureaucracy deserves mention. Bureaucrats in general have very long tenure. It is almost impossible to discharge them. The number of governmental employees discharged in the course of a year is trivial compared to the total number employed. The top bureaucrats were in place long before the current President was elected; they expect to remain in place long after the current President completes his term or terms of office. They have their fingers on the controls; they know where the bodies are buried. They can outwait the current President and the current legislature. Delay is an enormously effective instrument for this purpose and can be deftly exercised by bureaucrats.

Again, let us emphasize, we do not impute bad motives to government employees. On the contrary, the more dedicated a bureaucrat, the more determined he is that what he is doing is important for the country, the more persistent he is likely to be in making sure that his role is not reduced. An anecdote from William Safire's memoirs of his experiences as an aide to President Nixon brings home in an amusing way the problem of bureaucratic tyranny. It concerns President Nixon's attempt to eliminate the Board of Tea-Tasters. Said the President in the course of a message to Congress:

> "[T]he government since 1897 has had a special Board of Tea-Tasters. At one time in the dim past, there may have been good reason to single out tea for such special taste tests, but that reason no longer exists. Nevertheless, a separate Tea-Tasting Board has gone right along, at the taxpayer's expense, because nobody up to now took the trouble to take a hard look at why it was in existence. The general attitude was: It did not cost much, it provided a few jobs, so why upset the teacart?
>
> "That attitude should have no place in this government.

The taxpayer's dollar deserves to be treated with more respect."

This was only wasting about $125,000 a year, a drop in the slop-bowl, but there was a jocular, lifted-pinky sound to "Tea-Taster," and it was sure to be picked up by television newscasters. (David Brinkley, not ordinarily a Nixon Administration enthusiast, went for this with gusto.) As an object lesson in waste, with the scorn of commentators and columnists heaped upon them and the pressure of the Executive Branch demanding their removal, one might have thought the Tea-Tasters had had it. Enter some friendly Congressmen, solicitous of the views of some important tea importers, to point out that the board served a useful function in maintaining the quality of imported tea. That's nonsense. The standard Food and Drug Administration spot-check system used on all other imported foods is all that is needed, but the old board had tradition and tea industry pride going for it, plus influence on the House Ways and Means Committee. Specific legislation was needed from this committee to fold up the board, and it was not forthcoming. The President, under the threat of a writ of mandamus from the courts, had to reappoint the Tea-Tasting Board. There they sit today, a delightful anachronism, thumbing their noses at President and press, sipping their tea from the public trough, too small a boondoggle to raise an editorialist's ire, their longevity a testament to bureaucratic *chutzpah*.[5]

Today, a decade later, the Board of Tea-Tasters is still alive and well, under the auspices of the Food and Drug Administration.

Taken together, the three corners of the iron triangle guard against dismantling the functions of government. The tyranny of the status quo is strong and difficult to break.

WHAT CAN BE DONE?[5a]

Voluntary transactions in the economic market may have effects on third parties for which these third parties are neither compensated—

if the effects are bad—nor have to pay—if the effects are good. This phenomenon—frequently termed "market failure"—has been a major argument used to justify government intervention in the market-place. The most obvious example is pollution. We can all agree that clean air and clean water are desirable. But how are we to achieve specific ends without broadening government powers beyond a commonly perceived specific need? We must recognize that the problem arises when government engages in any activity, including activity intended to correct market failure. There, too, some get benefits without paying the costs, while others pay the costs without getting benefits. And, as already noted, those who get benefits without costs have a great political advantage over those who pay the costs without getting any benefits. The latter are in practice nearly helpless to do anything about it. As a result, market failure, while it does occur, is far less extensive, and generally less harmful, than government failure.

As we have seen, our elected representatives in Congress have been voting larger expenditures year after year—larger not only in dollars but as a fraction of the national income. Tax revenue has been rising as well, but nothing like so rapidly. As a result, deficits have grown and grown. In addition, the tax system has become ever more complex and cumbersome. At the same time, the public has demonstrated increasing resistance to higher spending, higher taxes, and higher deficits. Every survey of public opinion shows that a large majority believes that government is spending too much money, that the government budget should be balanced, and that the tax system, particularly the personal income tax, should be simplified.

How is it that a government of the majority produces results that the majority opposes?

The paradox arises because there is no effective bottom line for government. We are ruled by a majority, but it is a majority composed of a coalition of minorities representing special interests—2 percent in favor of a particular governmental measure will vote for a representative on the basis of how he votes on that measure *regardless of how he votes on any others*, 3 percent in favor of another specific measure, and so on down the line. Some minorities are tiny but geographically concentrated, like producers of tobacco; some are sizable and geographically dispersed, like the elderly for whom Social Security is of overriding importance. Each minority may well lose more from measures benefiting other minorities than it gains from measures benefiting itself. Yet no minority has an incentive to be concerned about the *cumulative* effect of the measures passed. Even if it were willing to give up its own special measures as part of a package deal eliminating all such measures, *there is no way currently it can express that preference.*

Similarly, as Congressman Gramm put it, it is not in the interest of a legislator to vote against a particular appropriation bill if that vote will create strong enemies, while a vote in its favor will alienate few supporters. Each of us will be favorably inclined toward a legislator who has voted for a bill that confers a large benefit on us, as we perceive it. Yet who among us will oppose a legislator because he has voted for a measure that involves a large expenditure but will increase the taxes on *each of us by only a few cents or a few dollars?* When we are among the few who benefit, it pays us to keep track of the vote. When we are among the many who bear the cost, it does not pay us even to read about it.

The result is a major defect in the legislative procedure whereby a budget is enacted and taxes are levied: each measure is considered separately, and the final budget is the sum of the separate items, limited by no effective predetermined total. That defect will not be remedied by Congress itself. One attempt after another at reforming the budget process and simplifying the tax system has failed. It simply is not in the self-interest of legislators, as they perceive it, to remedy it.

The defect cannot be remedied by the President. He can veto an appropriation measure as a whole but not individual items within the measure. The members of Congress know that, and they bury the items the President is known to object to in a broad measure containing items he favors, items that are regarded as essential to the continued operation of the government. The result is a game of

Chicken—such as produced a temporary halt on November 20, 1981, to all but the most essential activities of the U.S. government. President Reagan vetoed a bill containing appropriations greatly in excess of the amounts that he had proposed. As of 12:01 on November 21, 1981, it became technically illegal for the federal government to spend any money—something that many of us cheered. Needless to say, a compromise was quickly worked out to permit the government to continue churning out checks.

The President's ability to remedy this defect would be greatly strengthened if he could veto individual items in congressional measures. Governors of most of the states now possess such an item veto, subject, of course, to being overridden by the legislature, generally by a two-thirds vote. It will take a Constitutional Amendment to give the President a similar power.

The Constitution of the United States was conceived precisely as a way of making a package deal of the kind that is currently needed. There is hardly a provision in the original Constitution that would have been accepted separately by the requisite number of original States required to make the Constitution effective (nine states out of thirteen)—or, for that matter, even by a simple majority of the original Thirteen States. By balancing nicely the advantages and disadvantages of various provisions to different states—granting, for example, the large states more representation in the House of Representatives, but the small states equal representation in the Senate—the framers of the Constitution produced a package deal that all of the original Thirteen States ultimately adopted.

Similarly, Amendments to the Constitution are ways of packaging deals. Consider the First Amendment: "Congress shall make no law respecting an establishment of religion, or prohibiting the free exercise thereof; or abridging the freedom of speech, or of the press; or the right of the people peaceably to assemble, and to petition the Government for a redress of grievances."

There is nothing specified by this amendment that Congress could not achieve without it. Congress could deal, for example, with each proposed restriction on free speech separately, and decide in each case to pass "no law . . . abridging the freedom of speech." Why then was the amendment passed? In this case, to prevent majorities on individual issues from overriding a majority composed of minorities. A majority of us might well be willing to vote to abridge the right of many unpopular minorities: communists, fascists, preachers of free love, Moonies—the list could be extended indefinitely. All of us, however, would oppose strongly having our right to speak abridged when we are members of a minority. If each case were considered separately, no doubt many laws abridging freedom of speech would be passed. Combine all the cases in a package, and a large majority favors freedom of speech for all—the *benefit* to each of us as members of a minority more than compensates for the *loss* of our ability, when we are members of a majority, to restrict the speech of others.

These considerations have led many of us to conclude that the only way to get an effective package deal that will stop the growth of government and ultimately reduce its role, and that will simplify and reform the tax structure, is through Constitutional Amendments.

BALANCING THE BUDGET AND LIMITING SPENDING

✗ A Constitutional Amendment requiring the federal government to balance the budget and limit spending has been working its way through the Congress. The requirement to balance the budget will require a legislature that votes for spending also to vote for tax increases. The requirement to limit spending will require one program to be measured against another program.

The Senate passed such an amendment on August 4, 1982, by a vote of 69 to 31—two more than the two-thirds vote required for approval of a Constitutional Amendment. The approval was bipartisan: 47 Republicans, 21 Democrats, and 1 Independent voted for the amendment.

The House Democratic leadership tried to prevent a vote on the amendment in the House before the November 1982 elections. However, a discharge petition forced a vote on it on October 1, the last full day of the regular session. The amendment was approved by a majority (236 to 187), but not by the necessary two thirds. Again, the majority was bipartisan: 167 Republicans, 69 Democrats. In view of its near passage and the widespread public support for it, the amendment has been reintroduced and remains a live issue.

The amendment adopted by the Senate is as follows:

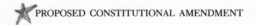 PROPOSED CONSTITUTIONAL AMENDMENT

SECTION 1. Prior to each fiscal year, the Congress shall adopt a statement of receipts and outlays for that year in which total outlays are not greater than total receipts. The Congress may amend such statement provided revised outlays are no greater than revised receipts. Whenever three-fifths of the whole number of both Houses shall deem it necessary, Congress in such statement may provide for a specific excess of outlays over receipts by a vote directed solely to that subject. The Congress and the President shall, pursuant to legislation or through exercise of their powers under the first and second articles, ensure that actual outlays do not exceed the outlays set forth in such statement.

SECTION 2. Total receipts for any fiscal year set forth in the statement adopted pursuant to this article shall not increase by a rate greater than the rate of increase in national income in the year or years ending not less than six months nor more than twelve months before such fiscal year, unless a majority of the whole number of both Houses of Congress shall have passed a bill directed solely to approving specific additional receipts and such bill has become law.

SECTION 3. The Congress may waive the provisions of this article for any fiscal year in which a declaration of war is in effect.

SECTION 4. Total receipts shall include all receipts of the United States except for those derived from borrowing and total outlays shall include all outlays of the United States except those for repayment of debt principal.

SECTION 5. The Congress shall enforce and implement this article by appropriate legislation.

SECTION 6. On and after the date this article takes effect, the amount of Federal public debt limit as of such date shall become permanent and there shall be no increase in such amount unless three-fifths of the whole number of both Houses of Congress shall have passed a bill approving such increase and such bill has become law.

SECTION 7. This article shall take effect for the second fiscal year beginning after its ratification.

This amendment would achieve two related objectives: first, it would increase the likelihood that the federal budget would be brought into balance, not by prohibiting an unbalanced budget but by making it more difficult to enact a budget calling for a deficit; second, it would check the growth of government spending—again, not by prohibiting such growth but by making it more difficult.

The key provisions of this amendment are to be found in the first two sections. The first requires that Congress *plan* for a balanced budget and that the Congress and the President shall make sure that actual spending does not exceed planned spending. Note that nothing is said about assuring that actual *receipts* equal (or exceed) planned receipts. That is deliberate. An Administration can pretty effectively control spending, but it cannot exercise the same degree of control over receipts, which are affected much more by economic conditions. Let a boom develop, actual receipts will exceed planned receipts; let a recession develop, receipts will drop. The first section does not rule out such automatically produced surpluses or deficits. This is one of the important subtleties of the amendment. It avoids a rigidity that would be intolerable and harmful. It requires no year-by-year budget balance, but balance over the length, or course, of business cycles.

By itself, the first section would not directly limit the growth of government. It would simply require that taxes and spending go up together. The second section adds the necessary element. It provides that planned receipts may not increase from one year to the next by a greater percentage than national income. Under Section 1, planned spending must be less than or equal to planned receipts, and actual spending must be less than or equal to planned spending. Hence, limiting receipts limits spending. Moreover, if in any year Congress manages to keep planned receipts and spending below the maximum level, the effect is to lower the maximum level for subsequent years, thus fostering a gradual ratcheting down of spending relative to national income.

Another strength of the amendment is the provision for approving an exceptional increase in planned receipts (hence in planned outlays). Some earlier versions of the amendment called for requiring a two-thirds majority to approve an exceptional increase in spending. The amendment that passed the Senate requires only "a majority of the whole number of both houses of Congress." Nonetheless, we regard this version as stronger than the earlier ones, because the majority must vote for an explicit tax increase. It is harder to get a simple majority of Congress to approve an explicit increase in taxes than to get a two-thirds majority to approve an exceptional increase in spending.

The amendment is very much in the spirit of the Bill of Rights, the first Ten Amendments to the Constitution. Their purpose was to limit the government in order to free the people. Similarly, the purpose of the balanced-budget-and-tax-limitation amendment is to limit the government in order to free the people, in this instance from excessive taxation. Its passage would go a long way to remedy the defect in our budgetary process. By the same token, it would make it more difficult for supporters of ever-bigger government to attain their goals.

It is no surprise that a torrent of criticism has been loosed against the proposed amendment by people who believe that our problems arise not from excessive government but from the failure to give government enough power or enough control over us as individuals. It is no surprise that the Democratic Speaker of the House, Tip O'Neill, and his fellow advocates of big government tried to prevent a vote in the House on the amendment. He and others used all the pressure at their command to prevent its receiving a two-thirds majority.

It is no surprise, either, that when the amendment did come to a vote in the House, a substantial majority voted for it. After all, repeatedly in opinion polls more than three quarters of the public have favored such an amendment. Their representatives do not find it easy to disregard that sentiment in an open vote—which is why Democratic leaders tried to prevent the amendment from coming to a vote. When their hand was forced, they quickly introduced a meaningless substitute that was overwhelmingly defeated (346 to 77), but that gave some representatives an opportunity to cast a recorded vote for a token budget-balancing amendment while at the same time voting against the real thing.

Unfortunately, the criticism of the amendment by believers in big government has been reinforced by skepticism about the amendment's possible effectiveness by persons who otherwise share our basic outlook about the importance of limiting government in order to preserve and expand individual freedom. They say that the Congress and the President could now, without an amendment, reduce government spending and balance the budget. Yet, the fact is, they have not done so and show little sign of doing so. If the same Congress and the same President enact budgets that produce large current deficits and also approve a constitutional amendment to limit future deficits, they are hypocrites. Could such hypocrites be counted on to carry out the amendment if adopted?

Of course, they would be guilty of hypocrisy. We have long believed that Congressional hypocrisy and shortsightedness are the only reasons that there is a ghost of a chance of getting Congress to pass an amendment limiting itself. Most members of Congress will do anything to postpone the problems they face by a couple of years—only Wall Street has a shorter perspective. If the hypocrisy did not exist, if Congress behaved "responsibly," the amendment would not be needed. Congress's irresponsibility is the reason that we need an amendment—and hypocrisy is, ironically, the reason that there is a chance of getting the amendment passed.

Though hypocrisy may eventually lead to the passing of the amendment, hypocrisy will not prevent the amendment from having important effects three or four years down the line—and from casting its shadow on events even sooner. Congress will not violate the Constitution lightly. Members of Congress will wriggle and squirm; they will seek, and no doubt find, subterfuges and evasions. But their actions will be significantly affected by the existence of the amendment. The experience of several states that have passed similar tax-limitation amendments provides ample evidence of this.

No Constitutional provision will be enforced unless it has widespread public support. "Prohibition" (the Volstead Act) certainly demonstrated that. However, if a provision does have widespread support—as public-opinion polls show that this one does—legislators are not inclined to flout it.

Equally important, legislators will find it in their own interest to confer an aura of inviolability on the amendment. This point has been impressed on us by the experience of legislators in states that have adopted amendments limiting state spending. Prior to the enactment of such amendments, they had no effective defense against lobbyists urging spending programs—all of them, of course, for good purposes. Now they do. They can say: "Your program is an excellent one; I would like to support it, but the total amount we can spend is fixed. To get funds for your program, we shall have to cut elsewhere. Where should we cut?" The effect is to force lobbyists to compete against one another rather than, as now, against the amorphous and poorly represented body of taxpayers.

Why are we optimistic that an amendment will be passed? The reason is found in Article 5 in the U.S. Constitution, which requires that "The Congress, . . . on the application of the Legislatures of two-thirds of the several states, shall call a Convention for proposing Amendments." This is the one provision in the Constitution that bypasses Congress. And this provision is being effectively used by the supporters of an amendment. It takes thirty-four states to constitute "two-thirds of the several states." So far, the legislatures of thirty-two states—most recently, Missouri, on May 26, 1983—have called for a constitutional convention to propose an amendment to balance the budget. It will take only two more to make calling a convention mandatory on Congress. More than two states may so vote fairly soon.

Congress does not want to be bypassed. It will be—as it has been in the past—most unwilling to have to call a convention. To avoid having to do so, it will, we believe, send a constitutional amendment to the states for ratification. When it does so, we have no doubt that the requisite three-quarters of the states will ratify it in short order.

The pressure on Congress offers a danger as well as an opportunity. The danger is that in order to preserve its own flexibility, Congress will try to emasculate the amendment while appearing to satisfy public clamor. The amendment adopted by the Senate in 1982 avoided that danger. The meaningless substitute proposed by the House leadership shows how great the danger is. It will take continued vigilance to ward off this danger.

The opportunity is no less real than the danger. There is every prospect today of an outcome that none of us would have regarded as at all likely as recently as five years ago. We predict that by the mid-1980s, a Constitutional Amendment will have been adopted that will have the effect of limiting federal spending and eliminating deficit financing.

AN ITEM VETO

🖈 A succession of Presidents, Democrats and Republicans, have expressed frustration at being required to approve or veto congressional measures as a whole. A President cannot pick and choose, approving some items and vetoing others.

The Congress is naturally opposed to an item veto because it would strengthen the power of the President relative to the power of the Congress. Their objection, however understandable, seems to us to have little weight under current conditions. The President and Vice President are the only federal officials elected by the people *as a whole*. They are the only ones who have any political incentive to represent the general interest as opposed to the interests of particular sections of the country. Moreover, every such proposal for a presidential item veto provides for an override of a veto by the Congress, generally by the same two-thirds majority currently required to override a veto, so no absolute power would in fact be conferred on the President.

Experience in the great majority of the states in which the governor now has an item veto does not suggest that it enhances unduly the power of the executive relative to the legislature. We know of no pressure from citizens within any of the states to repeal the item veto. There, too, the tyranny of the status quo is at work.

⭐ Needless to say, a President could use the item veto to prevent a reduction in the scope of government or to prevent expansion. But it would be politically profitable for him to do so only if the public at large wanted to increase rather than reduce the size of government. We believe that it is highly improbable that Americans will want this in the foreseeable future. In any event, if it so happened, that sentiment, too, should be capable of being effective in a democracy.

⭐ Support for an item-veto amendment has been growing. Senator Alan Dixon has introduced a bill proposing a Constitutional Amendment providing for an item veto. *The Wall Street Journal* has editorially supported the proposal. The movement is still in its early stages, but it will grow.

A FLAT TAX

Every President, as far back as we can remember, has denounced the complexity of the tax system, particularly the personal income tax, and promised to recommend measures to simplify it. Jimmy Carter, during his successful 1976 campaign for the presidency, described the country's tax system as "a disgrace to the human race" and pledged "comprehensive tax reform"—a pledge, needless to say, that he was unable to redeem after his election.[6] Instead, the tax system gets more complex every year. To add insult to injury, every IRS form and instruction now includes a Paper *Reduction* Act Notice: "We ask for this information to carry out the Internal Revenue laws of the United States. We need it to ensure that you are complying with these laws and so that we can figure and collect the correct amount of tax.

You are required to give us this information." A strange way to reduce the use of paper!

The result boggles the mind. As Robert E. Hall and Alvin Rabushka note, "The entire Code of Federal Regulations, all general and permanent laws in force in the United States, has 50 different titles filling more than 180 volumes. Title 26, the Internal Revenue Code, is responsible for 14 of these volumes, of which 8 are just for the income tax. Title 26 occupies 14 inches of library shelf space. The eight volumes for the income tax fill 5,105 pages, cost $65.00 per set, and weigh 12 pounds 2 ounces."[7]

In our book *Capitalism and Freedom*, first published in 1962, we recommended as a substitute for the existing personal income tax "a flat-rate tax on income above an exemption, with income defined very broadly and deductions allowed only for strictly defined expenses of earning income." Twenty years ago, this suggestion was dismissed as radical, impractical, and visionary.

But circumstances alter cases—and circumstances have changed. Three changes in particular have rescued the flat-tax idea from the limbo of good but impractical ideas. The most important change has been the tripling of prices from 1962 to 1982. Inflation subjected tens of millions of people to tax rates that they had earlier regarded as applying only to the "rich." Simultaneously, the public became more cynical about the income tax. "Soak the rich" has retained its dema-gogic appeal, but the conviction that the existing highly graduated income tax does in fact "soak the rich" has eroded sharply. Indeed, it has eroded even more sharply than the facts justify. The wide publicity that was given to the small number of persons who reported more than $1 million of gross income yet paid no tax concealed from view the much larger number of such returns that *did* pay very large taxes. Finally, the income tax law became more and more complex: the number of volumes of the Code of Federal Regulations devoted to the personal income tax went from one in 1954 to eight and one half in 1982; the number of pages from 957 in 1954 to 5,105 in 1982.

An article in the December 10, 1981, *Wall Street Journal* by Robert Hall and Alvin Rabushka triggered the current surge of interest in the flat-rate tax. As they report in the book they subsequently published on the flat tax, that article was followed by "editorial endorsements in the *New York Times*, the *Washington Post*, and the *Christian Science Monitor*. . . . Between February and June [1982], members of Congress introduced nearly a dozen flat-tax bills."[8] Unfortunately, not everything called a flat tax is specifically that. A true flat-rate tax has two components: first, a single tax rate that is applicable to everyone and to the whole of the tax base; second, a tax base that is equal to total income, with no deductions except personal exemptions and some strictly defined expenses that relate to earning the income.

Some of the bills labeled "flat rate" that have been pouring into the legislative hopper do provide for a true flat rate, notably a bill introduced into the House by Republican Representative Philip Crane of Illinois, and a somewhat different one introduced into the Senate by Democratic Senator Dennis De Concini of Arizona. However, most so-called flat-rate bills have only the label. They retain major deductions and keep graduated rates. For example, Senator Bill Bradley and Congressman Richard A. Gebhardt have introduced a much-publicized bill for a "flat-rate tax" that would retain deductions for contributions, interest paid on owned homes, state and local taxes, and income from Social Security and veterans' benefits. It also would have rates running from 14 percent to 28 percent—or a top rate that is double the bottom rate. While this is a far cry from a true flat rate, such proposals nonetheless appear attractive. They offer a compromise between the so-called left and right. The left might accept a lower top rate as the price of gaining a broader base. The right might accept a broader base as the price for gaining a lower top rate.

But, here, appearances are deceptive. Such a compromise is neither desirable nor feasible. Neither side would trust the other, and both would be right. If such a compromise were ever enacted, the left would go to work to raise the rates—and they would quickly be joined by persons on the right pleading fiscal necessity. The right would go to work to broaden the deductions—and they would quickly be joined by persons on the left pleading equity and social priorities. After all, that is how we got into our present fix. History *does* repeat itself.

In a true flat-rate tax, a rate of not more than 15 or 16 percent would yield the same revenue as the present system with its rates of 12 to 50 percent, assuming present personal exemptions were retained. If these exemptions were raised substantially—as they should be in view of the extent to which their real value has been eroded by inflation—a somewhat higher rate, perhaps 17 percent, would be required to raise the same revenue.

How is it that so much lower rates would yield as much revenue as the present much higher rates? The reason is that although the tax rates are steeply graduated on paper, the law is riddled with loopholes and special provisions, so that the high rates become window dressing. The income tax does indeed "soak the rich"—but that soaking does not yield much revenue to the government. It rather takes the form of inducing the rich to acquire costly tax shelters and rearrange their affairs in other ways that will minimize actual tax payments. There is a very large wedge between the cost to the taxpayer and the revenue to the government. The magnitude of that wedge was illustrated by the reduction in 1981 of the top rate on so-called unearned income from 70 to 50 percent. Despite ensuing recession, the taxes actually paid at rates of 50 percent and above went up, *not down*, as a result.

An even more dramatic illustration of how ineffective the personal income tax system has become as a way of getting revenue out of the rich—rather than simply soaking them—is provided by a comparison of incomes reported currently with those reported in 1929. In 1929, the top rate was 24 percent, levied on net taxable income in excess of $100,000. Nearly 15,000 returns reported such an income that year. From 1929 to 1980, our population increased by 87 percent, and per capita personal income in dollars increased nearly fourteenfold (mostly, of course, because of inflation). Hence, the counterpart in 1980 to the 15,000 returns that reported more than $100,000 in 1929 would have been 28,000 returns reporting taxable incomes of more than $1.4 million. We do not know how many such returns actually were filed in 1980. We do know that only 4,414 returns reported an *adjusted gross income* of $1 million or more in 1980. The number reporting a *net taxable income* of $1.4 million or more must have been far smaller. (Unfortunately, the Treasury Department's *Statistics of Income for 1980* does not classify returns by net taxable income, only by adjusted gross income, which is necessarily higher than net taxable income. In addition, the highest such class for which it reports the number of returns is $1 million or more.)

The enormous difference between 1929 and 1980 reflects the success of taxpayers in riddling the tax laws with loopholes and then taking advantage of them. The change since 1929 is not limited to millionaires—as is clear from a detailed comparison of returns in 1929 and 1980, income bracket by income bracket.

There is nothing either illegal or immoral about taking advantage of provisions of the law to reduce tax payments. As Justice Learned Hand said in a famous dissent: "Over and over again courts have said that there is nothing sinister in so arranging one's affairs as to keep taxes as low as possible. Everybody does so, rich and poor; and all do right, for nobody owes any public duty to pay more than the law demands: taxes are enforced exactions, not voluntary contributions. To demand more in the name of morals is mere cant."

In another case, Justice Hand said, "Any one may so arrange his affairs that his taxes shall be as low as possible; he is not bound to choose that pattern which will best pay the Treasury; there is not even a patriotic duty to increase one's taxes." [9]

The recent surge of interest in replacing the present income tax by a flat-rate tax has elicited a predictable reaction: the surfacing of an old myth. In the words of Tom Wicker, "the result [of a flat-rate tax] would be a massive redistribution of income, with more of the tax burden shifted from the rich to the poor and middle class." Contrary to Wicker, the poor, middle class, and rich would all gain from the substitution of a true flat-rate tax for the present income tax. The poor would pay less tax because of higher personal exemptions. Many in the middle class would pay less tax because of a lower rate. Others in the middle class, as well as the rich, would pay more tax to the government, yet they would be better off. They would pay more because the lower rate would render present costly tax shelters unattractive. And they would be better off because the gain to them from being free to use their assets in the most productive way would be greater than the gain from tax avoidance. The total cost of paying the taxes plus avoiding the taxes would be less. Tom Wicker's mistake is his failure to recognize how large a wedge there is between the cost to taxpayers of paying and avoiding taxes, and the revenue received by the government.

The flat-rate tax is clearly a splendid idea. Nonetheless, it also arouses intense opposition from powerful special interests created by the existing tax system: recipients of so-called charitable contributions, homeowners, the housing industry, institutions financing housing construction, the myriad other producers and users of tax shelter schemes, tax lawyers and accountants, and, not least, politicians who raise campaign funds from special interests by promising to retain existing tax loopholes or, better, to create new ones.

Congress itself is a formidable lobby, indeed, but the surge of public interest in the flat-rate idea opens up the possibility of enacting a Constitutional Amendment. Such an amendment is, we believe, the only way to make a bargain stick in which the "left" accepts a flat rate in return for a broader base, and the "right" accepts a broader base in return for a flat rate. The time has come to take that step and outlaw the outrageous income tax from which we now suffer.

In *Free to Choose*, we proposed such an Amendment to replace the present Sixteenth Amendment, which authorized the income tax: "The Congress shall have power to lay and collect taxes on incomes of persons, from whatever sources derived, without apportionment among the several States, and without regard to any census or enumeration, provided that the same tax rate is applied to all income in excess of occupational and business expenses and a personal allowance of a fixed amount. The word 'person' shall exclude corporations and other artificial persons" (p. 307).

CONCLUSION

What a change in public opinion created, another change in public opinion can modify. We cannot return to our starting point of, say, 1900 or 1920. Much has been created in the past half-century that is worth preserving. But we have, in the same period, centralized government power excessively. We must now decentralize that power. We have permitted government to grow too large. We must now cut it back to size. The tyranny of the status quo makes it hard to do. But it can and must be done.

4

DEFENSE

We the People of the United States, in Order to form a more perfect Union, establish Justice, insure domestic Tranquility, provide for the common defense, promote the general Welfare, and secure the Blessings of Liberty to ourselves and our posterity, do ordain and establish this Constitution for the United States of America.

Preamble to the Constitution of the United States

THE FRAMERS of the Constitution wisely put "provide for the common defense" before "promote the general Welfare"—and promoting the general welfare meant something very different to them than it has come to mean in the past fifty years.

The first obligation of any government is to protect the country from foreign enemies. Unless the country is thus protected, it will be impossible for the government either to promote the general welfare or to secure the blessings of liberty. Hence, defense must take priority over every other function of government along with the equally basic function of insuring "domestic Tranquility."

Yet, in the past two years the controversy about how much to spend on defense has proceeded as if the issue involved *were equity rather than security*—whether it is "fair" for expenditures on defense to be increased while expenditures on specific welfare programs are held constant or decreased, whether welfare is getting a "fair share" of the total or is being starved to feed defense.

We are not ourselves defense experts. We do not know what is the right amount of money to spend in order to assure the safety of our country. We *do* know that the issue of defense should not be decided in terms of "fairness" or "equity" but entirely in terms of security.

One way to judge the adequacy of spending is to compare current spending on defense with earlier levels after adjustment for changes in prices. As Figure 4.1 shows, defense spending trended downward from 1952 to 1979, interrupted only by sharp rises during the Korean and Vietnam wars. Real defense spending averaged 8 percent less from 1973 to 1979 than from 1955 to 1965, even though the threat to our security was far greater. By the late 1970s, the unquestioned nuclear supremacy we had enjoyed earlier had evaporated. In addition, the Soviet Union had greatly strengthened its conventional forces on the ground, on the sea, in the air.

Concern over the state of our defenses led President Carter to recommend a sharp increase in military spending during his last two years in office. Candidate Reagan made strengthening our defenses a major plank in his platform. President Reagan has been successful in translating that promise into reality. As a result, real defense spending rose rapidly in 1981 and 1982. Even so, by 1982, spending was only back to the level of the early 1960s.

THE CURRENT DEBATE

The current debate has been misleading not only because it emphasizes equity rather than security, but also because it gives a false impression of the role of military spending in the federal budget. Anyone who followed that debate solely in the headlines would surely conclude that military spending is the chief villain in generating high

FIGURE 4.1: **Defense Spending in Constant (1982) Prices, 1952–1982**

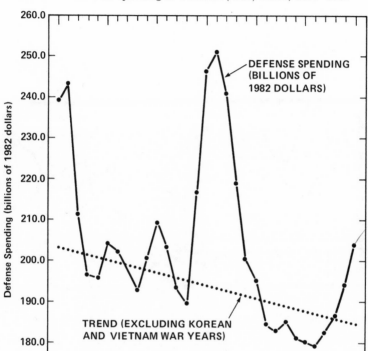

taxes and high deficits. Yet, as Figure 4.2 shows, that is totally false.

In 1956, after the Korean War and before our involvement in Vietnam, spending on defense (including veterans' benefits) amounted to 13.0 percent of the national income. All other federal spending amounted to 7.6 percent. Currently, defense spending, even after the Reagan sharp rise, amounts to only 8.4 percent of national income, while other spending is at an all-time high of 22.9 percent.

Compare our situation today with that before World War II. In 1940, defense spending amounted to only 3.6 percent of the national income; total federal spending amounted to 12.5 percent. The large

FIGURE 4.2: **Defense, Nondefense, and Total Federal Spending as a Percentage of National Income, 1952–1982**

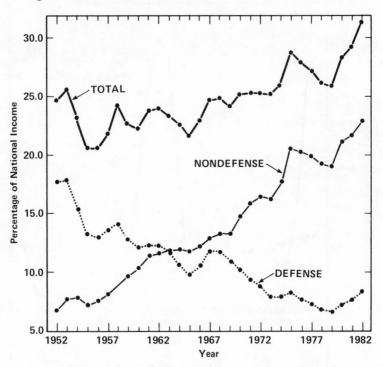

residual private sector enabled military spending to multiply rapidly to a peak of 48.5 percent of the national income in 1944, pushing total federal spending to a peak of 52.4 percent.

Given that federal spending already amounts to nearly one third of the national income and that three fourths of that is for nondefense, what leeway do we have today? The current debate shows how difficult it is politically to reduce nondefense spending, despite widespread disillusionment with much of that spending—and despite general support for a strong national defense. Actual or imminent hostilities would doubtless make it easier to cut nondefense spending, but by how much and how fast? How realistic is it to suppose that over four years we could repeat the World War II feat of *raising* military spending by 45 percent of the national income?

This analysis is not relevant in the event of a nuclear war. Such a war would be over in days or weeks and would have to be conducted with forces in being. We must prevent such an outcome—and by means other than national surrender. But the analysis is certainly highly relevant to the pressure that we can exert on the Soviet Union to engage in meaningful arms control or to avoid an arms race. They are right to regard us as a paper tiger.

DEFENSE VERSUS WELFARE

The Soviet Union is the immediate danger perceived by Americans. Yet it is not the real threat to our national security. The real threat is the welfare state, as C. Northcote Parkinson pointed out nearly a quarter of a century ago in commenting on the decline of Britain as a world power:

> Success in the modern age is to be measured by one's ability to give the minimum of effort to one's career and extract the maximum of subsidy from the state. To these ends a new generation was to devote itself, leaving the British empire to collapse more suddenly and more completely than any undefeated empire of the past; an example to the world of what excessive taxation can bring about and in how short a time. . . .
>
> The contrast between high taxable capacity and low taxes is a sign of latent strength and one not wasted on the world at large. Nor will rival powers fail to notice the high level of taxation maintained today in countries like Britain and France. Neither country, they conclude, will ever fight again except in defending its frontiers. A country so placed, with no visible margin of strength, can have only a dwindling influence in international affairs. That such a toothless country will do anything to

extend or even secure its wider interests is believed by nobody. It can do little even to maintain the peace. For most purposes it can be simply ignored.

The first effect, then, of a high rate of peacetime taxation is to reduce a country's influence in world affairs. The second effect is to be measured in the loss of individual freedom.[1]

These comments are as applicable to the United States today as they were to Britain and France when Parkinson wrote. The growth of the welfare state has increasingly absorbed the taxable capacity of the nation and is inexorably driving the United States into that state of impotence in international affairs that Parkinson rightly ascribed to Britain. We are convinced that Parkinson has more to contribute to the debate about how to insure the future security of the nation than do either Kremlinologists or military experts.

It is also true, however, that spending for defense is at the expense of spending on other things. There is no free defense, just as there is no free lunch. The choice between guns and butter, as it is popularly put, is a very real choice. If we have more guns, we will have less of other things.

GUNS VERSUS BUTTER

What the Parkinson analysis indicates is the difference between increasing defense spending at the expense of spending in general and at the expense of spending by government in particular. Why should it be easier, as it apparently is, to increase defense spending at the expense of spending in general, rather than at the expense of *other kinds* of government spending?

The basic reason goes back to the advantage of market arrangements over political arrangements as a way of organizing resources. If defense is expanded relative to spending in general, the burden is spread thinly over the populace. Even more important, each taxpayer separately can adjust his spending to the higher tax he must bear to finance national defense. He can tailor the adjustment to his own taste, spreading it thinly over all the items to which he devotes his income, or concentrating it on whatever category of spending he regards as most readily dispensable. No taxpayer has to accept the adjustment that has been reached by a political process. If the question is defense versus other government spending, that decision must be made on the political scene. *It must be made explicitly, specifically, and in the same way for every person in the country.* The cut in nondefense spending to offset additional defense spending must also be made program by program. The result is that, as each program is considered, the special group that benefits from that program has the usual concentrated incentive to prevent that program from being cut to provide the funds for defense, while the general public has only a minor interest in making sure that that particular program is cut to provide funds for defense.

The path of least resistance for politicians is to finance additional defense by adding to government spending in general, rather than by reducing expenditures on other governmental programs. The tax increase required to pay for the extra spending generally takes the form of inflation—and so for a time is hidden. That simply reinforces the tendency for the political process to finance a disproportionate share of the increase in defense by adding to the burden on the taxpayer rather than by reducing other government spending.

WASTE IN DEFENSE

Our analysis does not in any way deny that there is much waste and misuse of resources in defense expenditures. Studies of private versus governmental bus systems, private versus governmental fire protection, private versus governmental garbage collection, private versus governmental clerical work, and so on, have all shown that whatever activity government engages in tends to cost roughly twice as much as the same activity carried out by private entities. The same inefficiency undoubtedly characterizes defense. If somehow or other defense could be organized by the private market, we could unquestionably get as good a defense as we are now getting for roughly half the present cost.

Unfortunately, we have never been able to devise a way to have defense provided by the private market. The problem is the standard free rider problem. If some of us were voluntarily to spend money on national defense, the benefits would accrue to the whole population, including persons who contributed nothing. We could achieve little unless most of our fellow citizens participated. However, there is no separate individual incentive for each person to do so. Moreover people hired to work or fight by private groups representing only part of the people might well behave differently from the same people hired to work or fight for the nation as a whole. These are the key reasons why defense must be provided by government. Through government we all enter, as it were, into a contract under which each of us agrees to contribute—provided everybody else also agrees to contribute.

The very large number of strictly private charitable, cultural, and educational societies organized on a nonprofit basis demonstrates that many activities that benefit persons other than those who contribute can be carried out through strictly voluntary arrangements. But these are all on a far smaller scale than providing for the defense of the nation. It would be literally impossible to arrange an activity of that size on a national scale except through the medium of government.

Simply contracting with private enterprises to produce military weapons or to provide services does not achieve the efficiency of completely private operation because of the one thing that is missing: *the bottom line of privately allocated cost.* The government officials who contract for private production or provision of services are not spending their own money. And the taxpayers whose money they are spending have no effective way to hold them accountable. The taxpayers are likely to learn about extravagance, waste, and overspending only when a scandal develops or, even more infrequently, a major study is made. The private enterprises selling military goods or services know that this is the case and they have every incentive—in terms of their own bottom lines—to make it in the self-interest of the government officials to buy their products and pay high prices for them. The steady stream of scandals about the procurement of military supplies amply documents this phenomenon.

Given that defense must be provided by government, we must reconcile ourselves to spending a great deal more on defense than would be necessary if defense could be organized privately. But we can keep that extra cost to a minimum. Excess cost in defense arises from two very different sources. One is straightforward waste, inefficient ways of doing things; the other is political influence—again, the iron triangle, this time in defense.

The magnitude of straightforward waste has been brought out sharply by a task force, headed by J. Peter Grace, that President Reagan appointed to examine inefficiency throughout the government. In a story on some of the task force's findings, *Time* reported:

> The most controversial of the recommendations, . . . are those designed to save more than $89 billion over three years in defense spending. Military pensions should be scaled back. . . . Generous cost of living adjustments have allowed some officers who retired ten years ago to make more than those of equal rank on active duty. . . . Even issuing payroll checks results in waste. Private businesses can do it for about $1 a check but it costs the army $4.20. The Grace commission also cites the operation of unnecessary military bases and the domestic proliferation of subsidized commissaries (six in Washington, D.C., alone) that were originally intended to provide shopping facilities for servicemen in remote outposts.
>
> Encouraging more competition in the procurement of spare parts could save $695 million in three years, the Commission says. It notes that less than 25 percent of aircraft parts are purchased through competitive bids.

One further comment in that story is worth quoting: "Many top officials in the government agencies, while welcoming and even putting into practice some of the free suggestions of such highly qualified management consultants, shook their heads at the political naïveté a few of the businessmen showed." Grace admitted that the recommendations were made "without any reference to the political problems involved."

Eliminating unnecessary military bases, or for that matter even closing down unneeded subsidized commissaries, is no easy matter. Few issues arouse more vigorous and determined action from a member of Congress than the threat to close a base in his district. His constituents recognize that the base brings somebody else's money into their district. As they see it, it is an unmitigated good that they are getting jobs mandated by the government and paid for by someone else—unless the base contains nuclear warheads or missiles, which some of them may consider an unmitigated evil. Similarly, a Congressman's judgment of what kind of military hardware is desperately needed to defend the nation depends too often on whether his district "happens" to contain a factory producing one or another kind of military hardware. It is no accident that factories producing military hardware and military bases are concentrated in the Congressional districts represented by Congressmen who were, or are now, members—or, even better, chairmen—of the committees overseeing the military.

These are examples of a much broader phenomenon. Political considerations enter into decisions about strategy and tactics—not just into decisions about how and where particular military activities are carried out. The iron triangle is as powerful in the military area as it is in the civilian area. Each military service has its own partisans in Congress; each has its own beneficiaries in the civilian world. For example, Bath Iron Works, a division of the Congoleum Corporation which builds cruisers and frigates for the Navy, has for the past four years "placed full-page advertisements in the *Washington Post* at $11,819 a crack (and $26,338 each, less frequently, in the *Wall Street Journal*), wailing about how we've allowed the U.S. Navy to decay while the Soviet Union has built the premier naval power on earth."[2] These advertising expenditures do not come solely from a public interest in our military might; they are clearly motivated also by the expectation of private gain.

Competition among the services is to some extent a good thing, because each has an incentive to point out the deficiencies in the proposals of the other, but it also means that decisions on military policy take the form of political gerrymandering—if Michigan gets to build tanks, then Louisiana gets to build airfields. In 1947, the previously separate Departments of the Army, the Navy, and the Air Force were amalgamated into a single Department of Defense in the hope of more effectively bending the special interests of the separate services to the general interest. It is by no means clear that this hope has been realized. The separate services largely continue to go their own way. Their representatives to the Joint Chiefs of Staff do not in practice, as they are supposed to in theory, shed their lifetime loyalty to a specific service. It can be argued, they keep the loyalty because separate forces need esprit de corps, a pride in the face of danger. But does that justify waste?

As we have seen in one area of policy after another, the question is one of incentive. As members of the separate services, their personal interests were linked with the interests of those services. They have advanced to the top by serving those interests effectively. Suddenly designating them as "joint chiefs" does not provide them with any incentive to act in the "joint" interest rather than the separate interest.

CONCLUSION

Defense involves much more than maintaining military forces in being or in reserves. Defense involves the whole of our foreign policy. The military force we need to protect our nation depends on the strength of our allies as well as of our potential opponents. It depends on our success in preventing threats to our security from arising and not only on meeting threats after they arise.

Defense involves also the whole of our domestic policy. The pride that citizens have in their country, their faith in the causes they may be asked to defend are as much a source of strength as the uniformed forces in being. These underlay the incredible mobilization of manpower and womanpower that was achieved in World War II—just as a lack of faith in the cause for which we were fighting, whether justified or not, condemned us to defeat in Vietnam. Similarly, the industrial strength of the nation is truly part of our first line of defense.

Many of these issues are, we hasten to say, beyond the scope of this book. But some are not. Success in taming inflation, reducing the size of government, controlling crime, and improving education will add to our economic strength, will enlarge the freedom of our individual citizens, and will strengthen the cohesion within the nation. These developments ultimately will contribute far more to improving our defenses and to disheartening our potential opponents than will reduction in the unquestioned waste that now exists in the Army, Navy, and Air Force. By all means, let us root out waste as best we can. But let us not, in the process, lose sight that a major need is to keep the United States a nation worth defending.

5

INFLATION

There is no subtler, no surer means of overturning the exist-
ing basis of society than to debauch the currency. The pro-
cess engages all the hidden forces of economic law on the side
of destruction, and does it in a manner which not one man
in a million is able to diagnose.

—John Maynard Keynes (1920)

DURING THE 1980 presidential campaign, both Democrats and
Republicans recognized that inflation was the nation's number one
problem. Throughout 1980, consumer prices rose at rates well in excess
of 10 percent, and "double-digit inflation" became a household term.
In the second quarter of 1980, consumer prices were more than 14
percent above their level a year earlier. By the end of 1982, inflation
no longer ranked as problem number one. Unemployment had taken
its place. That change reflects both President Reagan's greatest success and the major obstacle to his achieving other elements of his
program.

Neither inflation nor public concern about inflation was restricted
to the United States. As inflation reached double-digit levels, the tolerance toward inflation declined sharply everywhere. As a result, it

became politically profitable to put into practice measures to stem inflation. In country after country, inflation has by now stopped going up. In most countries it has started to come down substantially. Wherever that has occurred, recession and unemployment have increasingly replaced inflation as the major source of public concern.

A fundamental question is whether the success in stemming inflation that has been achieved in the United States, and in other countries, is a temporary phenomenon similar to other declines in inflation rates during the course of the post-World War II roller coaster of ups and downs. On that roller coaster, each peak in the rate of inflation was higher than the preceding peak, each trough in the rate of inflation was higher than the preceding trough. An encouraging sign *this time* is that inflation has fallen below its preceding trough. However, that encouraging sign is tempered by other signs that raise the question: Will inflation continue to come down and will it be held down, or shall we return to another wild ride on the roller coaster?

The sharp decline in inflation is undoubtedly the greatest success of the Reagan Administration. That success was achieved at great cost. First, inflation has declined as much as it has in part precisely because one of the four pillars of Candidate Reagan's economic program has not been carried out, namely his call for a "stable, sound and predictable monetary policy." Second, the side effects of the decline in inflation have made it far more difficult to achieve other basic elements of President Reagan's program. The decline in inflation has been accompanied by economic instability, wide fluctuations in interest rates, and a sharp increase in unemployment. These have become major obstacles to success in holding down government spending, reducing tax rates, preventing large government deficits, and proceeding rapidly and effectively toward further deregulation of commerce and services. Third, a monetary explosion from mid-1982 to mid-1983 has produced an overheated economy that threatens to erupt in a renewed surge of inflation. The Federal Reserve System's attempt to offset that monetary explosion threatens a premature end to economic expansion and renewed recession in 1984. If recession does recur as early as the first or second quarter of 1984, the combination of higher inflation and higher unemployment would pose a serious threat to the reelection of President Reagan.

WHY HAS INFLATION COME DOWN SO SHARPLY?

One popular explanation of inflation attributes it to increases in the prices of specific goods and services—such as the sharply higher price of oil after the emergence of OPEC or rises in specific wages or prices, which are attributed to monopolistic trade unions or monopolistic producers. Despite its seeming plausibility, this explanation is basically false, although not wholly so. Inflation refers to the price level in general, not to the prices of particular goods and services. Higher oil prices may lead people to spend more money on oil. But if so, they have less to spend on other goods, which leads to downward pressure on the prices of those goods. The downward pressure offsets the upward pressure on oil prices, so that the price level in general need not be affected. However, most prices are slow to adjust. Hence, a sudden upward jump in the price of a product that is widely used, such as oil, may temporarily raise the level of inflation before the offsetting downward pressure becomes effective. That lagging behind events is the element of validity in the argument that rises in particular prices cause inflation.

Just as the rise in the price of oil in the 1970s was given much of the blame for the increase in inflation, so the decline in the price of oil in 1982—thus far, rather minor—has been given much of the credit for the sharp decrease in inflation. It may well be that the drop in the price of oil did in fact lower inflation for a short time, but that was both a minor and a temporary factor. The lower price of oil reduced spending on oil, which gave the community more funds to spend on other items, putting upward pressure on their prices. Relative prices—the price of oil relative to other prices, the wages of one type of labor relative to the wages of another type—are one thing; the general price level is a very different thing.

In *Free to Choose*, we noted that the basic source of inflation is always and everywhere a more rapid increase in the quantity of money than in the quantity of goods and services produced. Similarly, we stressed that the only way to reduce inflation is to reduce the rate of increase in the quantity of money.

The accompanying chart, Figure 5.1, illustrates the relationship between monetary growth on the one hand and inflation on the other. The solid line shows the growth of the money supply (as measured by M1 which is equal to currency plus transferable deposits) over one-year periods—from the first quarter of one year to the first quarter of the next, the second quarter to the second quarter, and so on. A one-year period averages out the shorter swings, but it leaves two notable features: an upward trend in the rate of monetary growth over the more than two decades covered by the chart and wide fluctuations around that trend.

The rising, and unstable, monetary growth has been the major immediate cause of the even more sharply rising, and even more unstable, inflation in consumer prices depicted by the dashed line. There is a long delay between changes in monetary growth and their effect on the rate of inflation. Hence, the inflation rate is plotted to correspond to a date two years later than the monetary growth rate in order to allow for the time it typically takes for a change in monetary growth to work through to the rate of inflation.

Note that the two dotted trend lines are very close together, although somewhat steeper for inflation. This relation has been experienced over and over again across the centuries in every part of the globe. Note also that the fluctuations about the trend are closely related. Even so, they are by no means identical. Some forces affect inflation without affecting the money supply, and conversely some forces affect the money supply without affecting inflation. For exam-ple, the rise in oil prices in the 1970s and some bad harvests partly explain the sharper rise in inflation in the late 1970s than in mone-tary growth two years earlier. Similarly, the end of those temporary effects partly explains the subsequent sharper fall in inflation. Tem-porary and random disturbances can also affect the money supply.

But all in all, the broader movements of inflation invariably follow the broader movements in the money supply.

The proposition that inflation is a monetary phenomenon is the beginning, but not the end, of understanding why inflation occurs. A full understanding requires investigating *why* the quantity of money rises rapidly sometimes, slowly at other times, and declines at still other times.

Changes in the quantity of money have come from many sources. When monetary systems were linked to gold or silver, discoveries of new sources of the metals increased sharply the quantity of money in existence. For example, after the Spaniards discovered large stocks of silver and gold in the New World, a sharp increase in the flow of the precious metals to Europe produced a price revolution. Similarly, the California and Australian gold discoveries in the late 1840s and early 1850s produced a period of inflation in the 1850s and 1860s. The perfection in the 1890s of the cyanide process for extracting gold from low-grade ore led to a flood of gold from South Africa that produced inflation from the 1890s up to the outbreak of World War I.

No country in the world today bases its money on a precious metal. We have what economists call a fiduciary money, in which the quantity of money is under the control of governmental monetary authorities. This feature of our money is the reason why government deficits *can* cause inflation, although not all deficits do. If a deficit is financed by borrowing from the public, it does not cause inflation. It has other bad effects, but it does not cause inflation because it simply substitutes government spending for private spending. Funds borrowed from the public are not available for the public to spend; instead, the government spends those funds. On the other hand, a deficit that is financed by creating money—either by the printing press or by accounting entries—has very different effects. In that case, government spends more dollars without anybody else spending fewer. The result is upward pressure on prices.

The creation of money to finance budget deficits is one reason governments favor inflation. But two other reasons have been even

FIGURE 5.1: **Inflation Follows Money: Percentage Change from Same Quarter One Year Earlier in the Quantity of Money and in Inflation Two Years Later, 1960–1983**

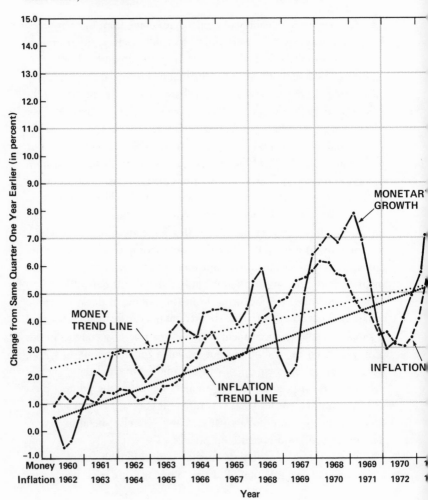

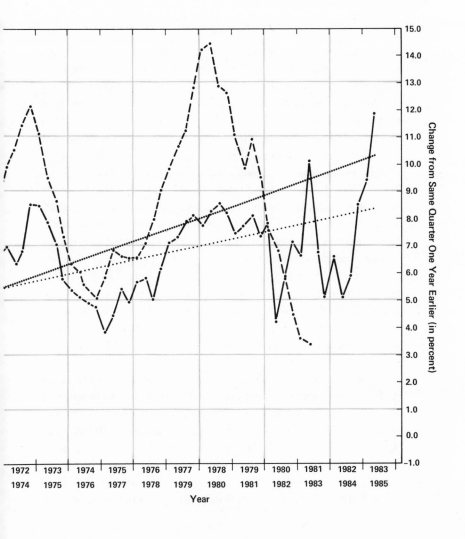

more important. First, inflation generates government revenue without any legislator having to vote for new taxes. As prices rise, government tax revenues tend to go up more rapidly than prices, because of bracket creep. Government spending on existing programs, on the other hand, tends to go up, at most, as rapidly as prices. As a result, inflation generates additional revenue that can be used to finance additional programs. Second, governments have resorted to inflation as a way to meet their commitment to promoting full employment. Whenever a recession develops, pressure arises for so-called expansive policies, which is to say policies of inflationary money creation. Such a policy does work for a time. However, as people catch on, the dose must be increased to be effective. A little inflation will provide a boost at first—like a small dose of a drug for a new addict—but then it takes more and more inflation to provide the boost, just as it takes a bigger and bigger dose of a drug to give a hardened addict a high. That process has produced the rising trend in inflation since World War II. At the same time, the reluctance of the monetary authorities to increase the doses as much as would have been needed to get the same boost in employment is one reason why successively *higher inflation has been associated with higher unemployment on the average, not lower unemployment.*

One of President Reagan's successes has been legislation that provides for indexing the personal income tax beginning in 1985, so that higher inflation will not automatically push people into higher income tax brackets. That measure, if it is not repealed, will remove much of the incentive for the Congress to resort to inflation as a way to increase tax revenues. For that very reason, some members of Congress opposed it, and some continue to agitate for its repeal. They profess to be concerned about big deficits that are said to be looming in future years. But this is camouflage. It stretches credulity to suppose that politicians who have always pooh-poohed deficits have suddenly become born-again budget balancers. They favor removing indexing because they remain what they have always been—big spenders. They recognize that widespread public opposition to budget deficits means that government spending is limited—at least, to some extent—by government revenues. It is not politically popular to vote for higher taxes. Hence, politicians want to restore the wonderful mechanism that raises taxes without anybody having to vote for higher taxes. That way, they hope to be able to resume their decades-old spending spree.

The recent decline in inflation, like earlier declines, is linked to a decline in monetary growth. Monetary growth peaked in the second quarter of 1978 and then started down, at first rather slowly. Inflation in consumer prices peaked nearly two years later, in the second quarter of 1980. The end of the four-year period of rising monetary growth ended a four-year period of even more rapidly rising inflation.

Inflation fell very rapidly—indeed, more rapidly than could have been expected simply from the decline in the rate of monetary growth. On the average over the past decades, a 1 percent change in monetary growth was followed two years later by a 1.2 percent change in inflation, as measured by consumer prices. This time, monetary growth fell by 3 percentage points from the third quarter of 1978 to mid-1982, while inflation fell by 9 percentage points from the third quarter of 1980 to mid-1983, or by 3 points for each 1 point decline in monetary growth.

In our opinion, three special factors explain why the decline in inflation was so rapid this time and why it exceeded greatly the decline in monetary growth. One is the fall in the price of oil, which temporarily speeded up the decline in inflation, just as the earlier sharp rise in the price of oil temporarily accelerated inflation.

A second factor is a defect in the measurement of the consumer price index for this period that exaggerated both the initial rise and the subsequent decline in inflation as measured by that index. The defect, which has since been corrected, involved giving undue importance to changes in interest rates in calculating the cost of housing. Although other price indexes, not affected by this defect, also show a more rapid decline than could have been expected from the decline in monetary growth alone, the difference is nothing like so large as for consumer prices.

A third factor that accounts for the sharper decline in inflation than in monetary growth is the extraordinary instability in monetary growth after 1979 and the associated instability in interest rates and the economy. Paradoxically, the increased instability in monetary growth followed an announcement by the Federal Reserve on October 6, 1979, that it was changing its operating procedures in order to be able to control the quantity of money more accurately. Unfortunately, the Fed changed its stated objective without adapting its rules, regulations, and techniques to its new objective. The result was that instability in monetary growth increased rather than decreased. President Carter's mistake in imposing credit controls in early 1980 further exacerbated the situation. The instability of monetary growth explains the erratic behavior of the economy and of interest rates: a six-month recession from January 1980 to July 1980; a twelve-month expansion from July 1980 to July 1981; a sixteen-month recession from July 1981 to November 1982; and a vigorous expansion since the end of 1982. The ups and downs in the economy and the wild gyrations in interest rates undoubtedly made the recession that started in July 1981 lengthier and more severe than it otherwise would have been. The combination of instability and a severe recession in turn made the decline in inflation greater than it otherwise would have been.

We have paid a high price for the rapid decline in inflation. Consider what would have happened if we had achieved President Reagan's monetary policy—a "stable, sound and predictable monetary policy." In that case, monetary growth would have declined gradually from a level of 8.5 percent in early 1980 to a level of perhaps 5 or 6 percent, which is where it actually stood in early 1982. It would have been expected to continue to decline thereafter.

The initial effect would have been a longer recession than the brief six-month recession that occurred from January 1980 to July 1980. The recession would probably have continued to the middle of 1981, ending with a level of unemployment somewhat higher, and a level of production somewhat lower, than was actually reached in mid-1980. However, a revival would then have started despite a reduced rate of monetary growth as declining inflation and developing confidence in steady monetary growth worked their magic. The resulting expansion would have been more like the typical postwar expansion which lasts about three years. That expansion would still be in progress as this book is being written and published. Instead, we had the short one-year expansion that occurred from July 1980 to July 1981. Unemployment would never have risen as high as it did. Output would never have fallen as low. We would not have experienced the extraordinary phenomenon of an absolute decline in per capita real income and real wages over a period of four or five years. Indeed, real income and real wages at the end of 1982 were lower than they had been ten years earlier, an almost unprecedented event in the history of the United States. A steadier monetary policy would also have meant lower and more stable interest rates. We conjecture that such an alternative pattern of monetary growth would have meant that short-term rates would have averaged 3 to 5 percentage points less than they actually did.

Lower interest rates and lower unemployment would inevitably have meant less government spending. A higher level of economic activity would have created higher revenues. On both scores, the deficit would have been lower. The much needed cuts in tax rates would have been able to exert their full supply-side effect, and there would have been far less resistance to further reductions in spending and in tax rates—reductions that are urgently needed. Finally, the occasion would never have arisen for the introduction or passage of a tax increase bill in 1982.

The cost of these benefits would have been a somewhat slower decline in inflation. Inflation would have declined perhaps by two or so percentage points less than it actually has. The benefits from a stabler economy, a higher level of employment, a lower budget deficit, and less pressure to increase government spending would have vastly outweighed the cost of a somewhat slower decline in inflation.

We can judge past policy only by what might have been—but we must live with the consequences of that policy. The question now is whether we shall even retain the one benefit—a more rapid decline in inflation. Will that decline turn out to be simply a brief downward phase, another gyration within the upward trend of recent decades, somewhat wider than usual but still a member of the same family as the earlier gyrations?

The monetary record of the past four years is hardly comforting. Monetary growth has been more unstable than in any other four-year period since the end of World War II. In addition, the monetary explosion since mid-1982 has pushed monetary growth to a new record high. As we wrote in April 1983, the

> money explosion puts the economy in a no-win position. Continued monetary growth at anything like recent rates would mean an upsurge in inflation in 1984 or 1985 at the very latest and higher long-term interest rates much sooner. . . .
>
> A drastic reversal that produced low or negative monetary growth . . . would produce a sharp if temporary increase in short-term interest rates, abort the economic expansion now in process and lead to a renewal of recession by early 1984.
>
> Even the least harmful course—prompt reduction in monetary growth to the Fed's own target limits (4 to 8 percent for M1) will, unless we are very lucky indeed, mean a rise in short-term rates, a slowdown in the expansion and a moderate increase in inflation.[1]

As we write this chapter in October 1983, the hour is much later, and additional damage has been done by the Fed's well-intentioned efforts to fine-tune the reduction in inflation and the consequent return to prosperity. The monetary explosion continued to July 1983 and has since been replaced by constancy or even decline. The Fed may once again be swinging from one extreme to the other, as it has so often in the past. Should that prove the case, renewed recession is highly likely in 1984. Alternatively, if the Fed resumes rapid monetary growth, double-digit inflation is highly likely by 1985. We shall be fortunate, indeed, to escape without experiencing either the one or the other.

PROSPECTS FOR THE FUTURE

The failure of monetary policy over the past few years makes it difficult to have confidence that inflation has really been conquered. Two broad scenarios seem possible.

1. The more favorable is that we shall have to suffer at least one more upswing of inflation, but can then keep inflation low. This scenario is rendered plausible by two facts: first, inflation currently is lower than its prior low point; second, the public is so fed up with high inflation that as it speeds up in 1984 or 1985, it will generate strong public pressures to stop it. The prospect for this scenario will be greatly enhanced if we are lucky—and renewed recession in 1984 is either avoided entirely or does not occur until late in the year. In that case, the odds are that President Reagan will be reelected and that his administration will continue to support a noninflationary policy.

Even in that case, there is no way to avoid a temporarily higher rate of inflation as a result of the delayed impact of the recent monetary explosion. But it is possible to keep inflation from again reaching double-digit levels. And there is no way to avoid a recession as a side effect of bringing inflation back down—a recession that would have been unnecessary but for the monetary explosion. But it is possible to keep the recession from being as severe as the 1981–83 one.

Under this scenario, inflation would come down over the next five years or so to a level below 5 percent and stay there. There would still be fluctuations in inflation, but these would be relatively minor. As the market learned to adjust to these fluctuations, the associated business cycles would become less severe, particularly if further tax decreases *and* restraint in government spending *and* deregulation strengthen the forces for real growth within the economy.

2. The second scenario is much less favorable. It would be likely to develop if a recession were to start in early 1984. In that case, the 1984 election would probably be fought in an environment in which inflation, interest rates, and unemployment all rise. Under those cir-

cumstances, President Reagan probably would not be reelected. Whichever Democrat is elected would be under strong pressure to revert to the traditional Democratic policy of spend and spend, tax and tax, elect and elect.

That policy would not bring an immediate return to double-digit inflation, but it would put the Federal Reserve under pressure to expand the money supply rapidly. Further inflationary pressure would undoubtedly develop. Given the public opposition to inflation, the administration in power would be strongly tempted to resort to price and wage controls. It would be ironic if a Democratic administration imitated the worst economic mistake that any modern Republican administration has made to date—namely, President Nixon's decision to impose price and wage controls in August 1971. The one thing we learn from history is that we do not learn from history.

The temptation to resort to price and wage controls would be great. The public memory is short. It will have been more than a decade since President Nixon's program provided such a striking demonstration of the defects of price and wage controls. Resort to price and wage controls might temporarily suppress inflationary pressure but, as in the early 1970s, the end result would undoubtedly be the collapse of the controls and a still higher inflation. It is fascinating to recall that consumer prices were rising at 4.5 percent in 1971 when President Nixon imposed price and wage controls to prevent "intolerable" inflation. Three years later, controls broke down and inflation reached 12 percent!

HOW TO ASSURE A STABLE PRICE LEVEL

It is easy to say how to assure a stable price level—just as it is easy to say how to cure drug addiction. Assuring a stable price level simply requires a "stable, sound and predictable monetary policy" that keeps the rate of monetary growth steady and low—just as curing drug addiction simply requires that the addict abstain from taking drugs.

WHY THERE IS A PROBLEM

Saying is one thing; doing is another. The members of the Federal Reserve System have long known how to assure a stable price level—just as the drug addict knows how he can be cured. They have proclaimed it repeatedly in testimony to Congress, public speeches, private conversation. Moreover, the Federal Reserve System has long had the power and the means to keep monetary growth steady and low—just as the drug addict has the recourse to abstain if he has the will and moral support.

Yet, the fact that the Fed knows what should be done—and apparently has the legal power to do it—does not mean that that power will be exercised. We now have had seventy years of experience showing that the forces determining how the Federal Reserve actually operates *do not generate stable monetary growth*. On the contrary, over the whole of its history, the Fed has been a source of instability rather than of stability. We have argued many times that the United States would have been far better off had the Federal Reserve System never been created. Unfortunately, it was created, and having been created, it has now achieved bureaucratic immortality. If left unchanged, it will continue to act as it has in the past.

In our opinion, the Fed acts as it does because it is a large bureaucracy that has no bottom line. The Federal Reserve System does not have to go to Congress to get appropriations. It prints its own money, so is free from any budgetary restraint. The people who are in charge of the Federal Reserve—the Board of Governors and the presidents of the twelve Federal Reserve Banks—are all appointed rather than elected. The presidents of the banks are appointed by the boards of directors of the banks, subject to approval by the Board of Governors. The members of the Board of Governors of the Federal Reserve are appointed by the President for a term of fourteen years and cannot be reappointed unless they are completing the unexpired term of a member who retired before completing his term. The chairman is appointed for a period of four years. *Reappointment of the chairman is the only effective bottom line that the Federal Reserve Board has.*

In Chapter 3, we discussed the law of bureaucratic inertia: Every large bureaucracy, government or private, is certain that the way it conducts its affairs is the only way that they can be conducted. We illustrated the law there with the Internal Revenue Service. The Federal Reserve provides an equally striking example.

In its seventy-year history, to the best of our knowledge, the Federal Reserve Board has never admitted error in any official statement—although some courageous officials at regional banks have done so. Doubtless there are exceptions—perhaps Senator William Proxmire should establish a Golden Purse award for authors of such admissions, to match his Golden Fleece award for wasteful expenditures. Changes in policy and procedure have of course occurred—mostly as a result of crisis pressures from outside. Occasionally, changes in policy occur from changes in personnel. Even more rarely, they occur from cumulative self-generated policies growing out of the work of the Board's own able professional staff, or the able professional staffs at some of the regional banks.

In 1975, Congress passed Concurrent Resolution 133, which expressed "the sense of the Congress" that the Fed "maintain long-run growth of the monetary and credit aggregates commensurate with the economy's long-run potential to increase production," and provided that the Fed "consult" Congress at regular intervals about its "objectives and plans" for monetary growth and "report to the Congress the reasons" for any subsequent departure from these objectives.[2]

At the time, we described this resolution as "perhaps the most important change [in the structure of monetary policy] since the banking acts of the mid-1930s," and, in justifying this judgment, wrote: "Though superficially innocuous [because it has no teeth], the resolution represents the first time since the Fed began operation in 1914 that the Congress has (1) specified monetary and credit aggregates as the Fed's immediate target, (2) enjoined it to produce steady monetary growth in line with output growth, (3) required it to state its objectives publicly in advance, and (4) required it to justify publicly any departure from them. All four elements are major changes. The Fed has shifted among alternative targets—monetary aggregates, interest rates, exchange rates; it has produced widely varying rates of monetary growth; it has never specified long-range numerical objectives and has decided its short-term objectives in camera, making them public long after the event; it has reported to Congress in vague terms that have resisted strict accountability."[3]

This judgment proved wide of the mark. The Federal Reserve had strongly opposed the resolution and had tried to prevent its passage. When it was passed, the Fed pledged cooperation, but then proceeded to undermine it so subtly and effectively that the resolution has proved to be a noteworthy minor step—rather than the major breakthrough we mistakenly interpreted it as being. James Pierce, who served on the research staff of the Board of Governors for many years, made a more accurate assessment of the likely effect of the resolution in 1977—two years after it was adopted—when he wrote: "Whatever can be said for Congressional supervision of monetary policy, it has not produced closer control over the monetary aggregates and it has not lessened the Fed's penchant for stabilizing movements in short-term interest rates. It appears safe to conclude that increased Congressional oversight has not altered the conduct of monetary policy."[4]

Figure 5.2 illustrates the departure of monetary growth from the Fed's announced targets from the fourth quarter of 1978 to the second quarter of 1983—the period covered by targets decided on during the incumbency of the present chairman, Paul Volcker. The Fed presents its targets for M1—currency plus transferable deposits—as a range of growth rates: for example, fourth quarter of 1978 to fourth quarter of 1979, 4 to 6.5 percent, the midpoint of which is 5.25 percent. We have taken the midpoints of these ranges and linked them together, so that on the line labeled "target," the point plotted for the fourth quarter of 1979 is 105.25, for the fourth quarter of 1980, 110.8 (105.25 times 1.0525), since the target range for 1979 to 1980 was the same as for 1978 to 1979, and so on. The line labeled "actual"

FIGURE 5.2: **Targeted and Actual Values for M1: Fourth Quarter of 1978 to Second Quarter of 1983**

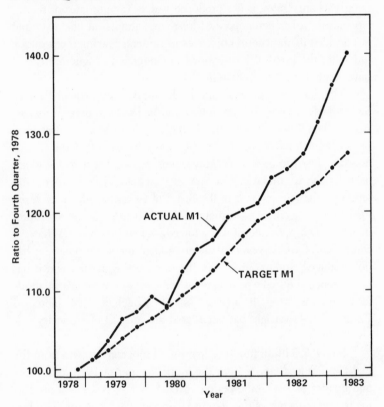

is simply the reported value of M1 for the quarter expressed as a percentage of the value for the fourth quarter of 1978. The inflationary bias of the Fed is clear.

The conclusion is inescapable: the achievement of a "stable, sound and predictable monetary policy" will require more than preaching to the powers that be. It will require a major change in the institutional arrangements for conducting monetary policy.

STRUCTURAL REFORM

One such change would be to separate the two functions that the Fed performs—namely, the regulation of individual banks and other financial institutions, and the control of the money supply. The regulatory function could be combined with that of the FDIC and the comptroller of the currency and exercised by a single governmental agency replacing the three present agencies. The money control function could be exercised by a small group placed within the Treasury Department. That would end the present division of responsibility for economic policy between the Treasury and the Fed. It would assure that a single agency would have full responsibility to recommend and conduct monetary as well as fiscal policy.

A still more fundamental change has been proposed by many people. It is to reestablish something like a gold standard, either by requiring the Federal Reserve to use the price of gold or sensitive commodities as a criterion in determining monetary growth, or more fundamentally by committing the government once again to buy and sell gold or silver or some other sensitive commodity at fixed prices. These policies are appealing because we tend to view history through rose-colored glasses. Prices were on the average stable during the nineteenth and early in the twentieth century. It is tempting to regard that stability as a sign of ideal monetary arrangements. However, stability *on the average* did not prevent wide fluctuations up and down in both prices and economic activity. Moreover, when the gold standard worked reasonably well in the United States, federal government spending, as we have seen in earlier chapters, amounted to only 3 percent of the national income. Today, it is ten times that much. The willingness of the federal government to allow its policies to be dominated by gold discoveries and other factors affecting the supply and demand for gold was one thing when it was spending 3 percent of the national income. It would be much less willing now. Moreover, a true gold standard makes sense only if it is international. There is no chance of *that* taking place currently.

There are two key objections to current proposals for linking the quantity of money to the price of gold or silver or to the price of sensitive commodities—one economic and one political. The economic objection is that changes in the money supply today do not influence the economy today. On the average, an increase in the rate of monetary growth today produces an increase in total spending by consumers and business only some six or nine months later. That increase in spending is first reflected in output and employment. Its effect on prices, as we have seen, typically does not occur for something like two years. As a result, using today's prices to determine today's monetary growth is like fighting the last war.

The political objection is in some ways more fundamental. The current proposals would not correct the major political defect of the present system. The power to determine how much money there is is too important a power to be entrusted to a few people sitting around a table in Washington who are not subject to election, not subject to dismissal, not subject to any effective political control. *Yet that is where the power now resides.* That is why we have long argued that it would be desirable to eliminate the discretionary power of the Federal Reserve. Requiring the Fed to buy and sell gold *at fixed prices* would eliminate their discretion. However, most proposals do not involve imposing that requirement. They would have the Fed use the price of gold or some other group of sensitive commodity prices as one among other *guides to policy* in the same way that it now uses the behavior of the price level or interest rates or industrial production. In that case, discretion would not be eliminated. The Fed would simply have an additional excuse—since it is no more likely to be successful in controlling the price of gold by policies such as it currently follows than it has been in controlling interest rates or the price level.

The appearance of wide backing for a gold standard, or its equivalent, is highly misleading, as was demonstrated by the 1982 report of a Commission on the Role of Gold in the Domestic and International Monetary Systems. The commission was established by the U.S. Congress and chaired by the Secretary of the Treasury. In the course of its hearings and deliberations, it became clear that "support of a gold standard" meant very different things to different people, and that only a very few favored a real gold standard in which gold would literally be used as money. The conclusion of the commission was that "The majority of us at this time favor essentially no change in the present role of gold." [5]

In *Free to Choose* we proposed as an alternative a constitutional amendment that would require the Fed to increase the quantity of money it issues at a fixed rate year in and year out. That seems to us a much better solution than a gold standard or similar arrangements. Absent such a constitutional amendment, the most promising alternative is legislation that would strip the Federal Reserve of the power to control the quantity of money and place that power within the Treasury system. That will not be easy to achieve. It will probably not occur until after there has first been a further resurgence of inflation—a resurgence so great that a change in the monetary structure will be seen as absolutely essential.

In the meantime, the one optimistic note is that the private market is creating arrangements that reduce both the harm that variable inflation imposes on the innocent public and the incentive for the government to resort to inflation.

The major development in the 1970s was the emergence of money market mutual funds. These enabled the small saver to escape the rigid ceilings that had been imposed on the rates of interest banks and thrift institutions could pay depositors—ceilings that were often lower than the rate of inflation. They also gave small savers an alternative to government securities that paid similarly low rates. In effect, savers were paying borrowers, whether banks or governments, for the privilege of lending to them if allowance is made for the effect of inflation. One result was to force the deregulation of banking, so that banks could compete with mutual funds. Another result was to reduce government's incentive to resort to inflation, since government, like banks, had to pay competitive interest rates.

Another development, still in only its formative stage, is futures markets in price index numbers. There have long been futures markets in commodities—wheat, corn, cotton, etc. These are markets in which you can arrange to buy or sell a commodity at a specified future date for a fixed price. By means of such markets, farmers, millers, manufacturers can protect themselves—they can "hedge"—against unexpected changes in prices. In the past decade or so, the scope of such markets has exploded. The end of the Bretton Woods System of fixed exchange rates led to the establishment of the International Money Market, which provides futures markets in foreign currencies—the British pound sterling, the German mark, the French franc, etc. The rapid rise in interest rates and the emergence of great instability in interest rates led to the establishment of futures markets in our own financial instruments: in government bonds, in other bonds, in U.S. Treasury bills, and so on.

Recently, markets have developed in stock market indexes. These differ from all the others in the absence of any real possibility of requiring delivery at the date specified in the contract. In all other markets, there is at least a possibility of doing so. In principle, a person who contracted to buy eggs at a specified price in December 1984 could, when December 1984 came, require the person with whom he made the contract to deliver the eggs; similarly for wheat or cotton or French francs or a U.S. Treasury bond. In practice, that almost never occurs. The contract is settled by the payment of cash: if the price at which you agreed to buy something is less than the current price, you are paid the difference; if it is higher, you pay the difference. With the futures markets in stock price index numbers, settlement is always in cash, never by the delivery of a bundle of securities whose prices are combined in calculating the index number (e.g., the 500 stocks whose prices enter *Standard and Poor's 500* index).

Preliminary moves are already in process to take the next step and introduce similar futures contracts in general price index numbers—for example, in the consumer price index that is widely used in wage contracts, in which wages are automatically adjusted from time to time for inflation. Such an index number is, in effect, the price of a standard basket of goods: a specified number (or fractional number) of eggs plus a specified number (or fractional number) of pairs of shoes, and so on through an extended list of commodities and services—just as the popular Dow-Jones stock price index is the sum of the prices of a specified number of shares of stock in each of thirty major companies.

A futures contract in the consumer price index will be an agreement to buy or sell a specified number of baskets of goods at a future date at a specified price per basket. If at that date the actual price is lower than the contracted price—that is, inflation turns out to be less than anticipated—the purchaser will pay the seller the difference in cash. Conversely, if the actual price is higher, the seller will pay the purchaser the difference.

Who will trade in such contracts? As in all futures markets, two classes of people: hedgers and speculators. You are, for example, the owner of a department store and are purchasing in the spring goods to be sold in the fall. If between the spring and the fall, inflation is less than you anticipate, you would lose; if greater, you would gain. You could protect yourself—hedge—against either loss or gain, by selling a consumer price index contract for an autumn date. If inflation is less than you anticipate, you will make a gain in the futures market that will offset the loss in your store sales; if inflation is greater, you will have a loss in the futures market that will offset the gain in your store sales.

Through such a set of markets—involving different kinds of price indexes to meet the needs of people facing different kinds of risks— persons could confidently enter into ventures that take a long time to complete without having to assume the risk that higher or lower inflation than they anticipate would bring loss or even ruin. Mr. A, for example, could enter into a contract at a fixed dollar price with Mr. B to build a factory that will take three years to complete; both can protect themselves against the risk of lower or higher inflation than they anticipate. Mr. A stands to lose if inflation is higher than he expects—since that would raise his costs. Accordingly, he would offset that risk by buying a futures contract in an index linked to building costs. Mr. B stands to lose if inflation is lower than he expects—since that would lower the market value of the factory. He would offset that risk by selling a futures contract in an index linked to the price of factories.

Both would be enabled to do so by the large body of speculators—people who specialize in assuming risks—who would be buying and selling not to offset opposite risks but as a way, in effect, of betting on their beliefs about whether inflation is likely to be greater or less than most participants in the market expect.

We have introduced this lengthy discussion of futures markets for two reasons. The first is this: we are skeptical that government is likely to provide such a satisfactory resolution of the problem of inflation that we can all make plans for the future in the confident expectation that we can know what the general level of prices will be when those plans mature. The one thing of which we are reasonably certain is that the future course of inflation is shrouded in uncertainty. The second reason is this: futures markets in price indexes seem to us the single private-market development that will do the most to reduce the harm from uncertain and unstable inflation. They will provide a mechanism that will enable long-range projects to be undertaken despite the uncertainty of inflation, that will enable ordinary people to protect their assets despite that uncertainty. By so doing, futures markets in price indexes will also remove the incentive for governments to resort to inflation and bring closer the day when a monetary reform can be adopted that will assure stable prices and thus render them unnecessary.

Like indexation in general, futures markets in price indexes are not, in and of themselves, a good thing. Far better is a world in which there is neither uncertainty about the future course of prices nor extensive futures markets in price index numbers. But given the present uncertainty about the future course of prices, the emergence of the futures markets is evidence of the incredible ingenuity of the private market to surmount the roadblocks to productivity and growth that are generated by the political market.

6

UNEMPLOYMENT, SMOKESTACK INDUSTRIES, TARIFFS

We have come to our present pass through the pursuit of the noble objective of "full-employment" by the wrong means. We have seized on policies with temporary and fleeting effects, resulting from the slowness of human beings to adapt to changing opportunities and elevated them into fundamental truths of economics.

—Samuel Brittan [1]

IF THE SHARP decline in inflation was President Reagan's greatest success, the accompanying sharp rise in unemployment was clearly his greatest failure. There is an important difference between the two phenomena. The decline in inflation to a level below the prior low point was a break in the long-term trend of the inflation roller coaster—see Figure 5.1, page 86. The rise in unemployment to a new peak of 10.7 percent of the labor force in December 1982 was a continuation of a long-term upward trend of the unemployment roller coaster, as Figure 6.1 (page 108) makes clear.

These phenomena were not special to the United States. In many countries around the world, notably in Great Britain, Germany, and Japan, inflation declined in the past several years to a level below earlier lows, and unemployment rose to new highs. In these countries, as in the United States, the decline in inflation was a break in a long-term trend, whereas the rise in unemployment was a continuation of a trend.

Everywhere, the decline in inflation has been welcomed, the rise in unemployment deplored. Everywhere, the rise in unemployment has been blamed largely on the measures taken to cure inflation—particularly restrictive monetary policy. Everywhere, it has prompted pressure for the same corrective steps: higher government spending to "create" jobs; expansive monetary policy; government assistance to declining firms and industries; "protection" against foreign competition. The widespread belief that the rise in unemployment is attributable to the measures taken to cure inflation is a misleading half-truth. The proposed remedies would do far more harm than good. They represent another dose of the drug that is largely responsible for the upward trend in both inflation and unemployment.

In this chapter, we shall examine the question why unemployment is so high, the meaning of the unemployment figures, the defects of the remedies—"jobs bills," subsidies to firms and industries, "protection"—and then turn to discuss some measures to alleviate unemployment that would do more good than harm.

WHY IS UNEMPLOYMENT SO HIGH?

As Figure 6.1 shows, unemployment in the United States, like inflation, has displayed an upward trend over the past three decades. And like inflation too, the unemployment rate has fluctuated widely around that upward trend. But there is an important difference. Inflation and unemployment move in the same direction over longer periods; they move in opposite directions over shorter periods. During economic expansions, inflation tends to rise, unemployment to fall; during recessions, inflation tends to decline, unemployment to rise. Since 1980, the short-term behavior has been painfully evident. Inflation has declined rapidly: from nearly 15 percent in April 1980 to only 4 percent by December 1982 (as measured by the change in consumer prices from the same month a year earlier). By contrast, unemployment rose from less than 6 percent of the labor force in mid-1979 to nearly 11 percent by the end of 1982.

This high level of unemployment reflects two very different forces: the reaction to disinflation and recession, and the long-term upward trend. The reaction to disinflation and recession is easy to explain. The long-term upward trend is more complex.

Disinflation inevitably produces a temporary rise in unemployment. The primary reason is the existence of long-term contracts that embody expectations of continued inflation. When such contracts— whether for employment or borrowing and lending or production of goods or construction—were entered into in 1978, 1979, and 1980, the environment was one of rising inflation. Persons entering into the contracts took into account not only the existing inflation in the wages, interest rates, and prices they agreed to, but also the likelihood that inflation would continue to rise. When inflation stopped rising and started to decline, these contracts were out of line with the existing situation. Moreover, there was great uncertainty about the future. Would inflation continue to decline? Or was this just another flash in the pan? The response was understandably an unwillingness to expand and enter into new ventures. There was a tendency for producers and consumers alike to retrench, especially those persons or enterprises who were stuck with terms that had turned out to be unfavorable.

The reaction was particularly severe on this occasion, and more severe in the United States than in some other countries, because of the greater instability in monetary growth. Monetary instability produces wide gyrations in interest rates and in economic activity and thereby intensifies the uncertainty that under any circumstances accompanies a shift to disinflation. Very much the same thing happened in Great Britain, and there too, the increase in unemployment was particularly sharp.

This is the element of truth in the claim that the high unemployment is a result of the economic policies adopted to cure infla-

FIGURE 6.1: **Unemployment as a Percentage of the Labor Force, 1950–1982 (actual and trend)**

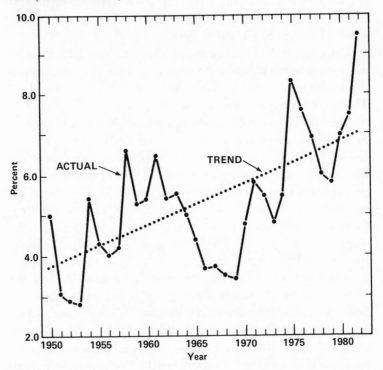

tion. A steadier monetary policy would have meant a slower decline in inflation—and also a smaller rise in unemployment. However, this effect was not very large. As Figure 6.1 makes clear, the rise in unemployment from 1979 to 1982 was larger, but not very much larger, than the similar rises during earlier recessions: 1953–1954, 1957–1958, 1969–1970, 1973–1975. The important difference is that it started from a higher level: an average of 5.8 percent in 1979, 4.8 in 1973, 3.4 in 1969.

The long-term upward trend in unemployment, and particularly its linkage to the upward trend in inflation, is less readily explained. It runs counter to the widespread belief that inflation and unemployment are alternatives—that inflation provides a stimulus to the economy that reduces unemployment, and that creating unemployment is a way to reduce inflation. That belief, which derives from the short-term inverse relation between inflation and unemployment, is only partly true even in the short run and is the reverse of the truth for the long run. Temporarily, higher unemployment is an unavoidable side effect of the monetary restraint that alone can reduce inflation—just as staying in bed is an unavoidable side effect of having your appendix out. But creating unemployment is not a way to reduce inflation—just as staying in bed is not a cure for appendicitis. There are many sources of increased unemployment that tend to raise rather than offset inflation. A prime example is OPEC's embargo on oil in 1973.

In our view, the upward trends in inflation and unemployment are partly cause and effect but mostly, the common result of the changes in the role of government documented in Chapter 2.

High inflation, especially if it is variable, tends to render the economic system less efficient. A fundamental function of a market price system is to transmit compactly, efficiently, and at low cost the information that economic agents need in order to decide what to produce and how to produce it—in short, how to employ resources. The relevant information is about *relative* prices—of one product relative to another, of the services of labor relative to the services of capital, of prices at present relative to prices in the future. But the information is transmitted in the form of *absolute* prices—prices in dollars and cents. If the price level on the average remains stable or changes at a steady rate, it is fairly easy to extract the signal about relative prices from observed absolute prices. But if inflation is volatile, moving up and down at irregular intervals, as it has been these past decades, it becomes hard to extract the signal about relative prices from absolute prices. Put it this way: the broadcast about *relative* prices is being jammed by the noise coming from broadcasts on *inflation*. At the extreme, the system of absolute prices becomes nearly useless, and economic agents then resort either to an alternative currency or to barter with disastrous effects on productivity.

Both the marked slowdown during the past decade in economic productivity—and hence in average real income—and the general upward trend in unemployment reflect in part the increased amount of noise in market signals.

The rising and variable rate of inflation is, as we showed in Chapter 5, itself primarily a result of the growing role of government and the political difficulty of legislating higher taxes to finance ever larger government spending. Other effects of the expanding role of government have, we believe, been even more important in raising unemployment both in the United States and elsewhere. One is the growth in government programs that reduce the costs of being unemployed or, in effect, that subsidize persons for not working. These programs must be financed by the productive activities of the community. So they have a double effect: they reduce the return from working at the same time that they reduce the cost of not working. They discourage work and encourage nonwork. These programs *do* have much to recommend them. They have eased the lot of many persons in economic trouble. But they also have their costs. And a major cost is surely a higher level of unemployment.

Consider an automobile worker who loses his job. He has been employed at a wage rate that is nearly double the average wage rate of all other workers in manufacturing. Understandably, he is reluctant to accept a much lower wage. Yet, if that is all he can command in an alternative activity, he will sooner or later have to do so. Without unemployment insurance and special unemployment benefits of various kinds, he would have to do so sooner. But with these benefits, he will be inclined for a considerable period to take a higher income by not working than he could earn by working. You cannot blame him if he chooses not to accept a low-paying job but instead keeps looking for a job that pays as much as he had been earning.

This is not a criticism of the persons who receive unemployment benefits or other forms of governmental assistance. So long as those programs are available, people are sensible to take advantage of them! Neither does it mean that those programs are necessarily undesirable. But it does mean that they impose a considerable cost on all of us over and above the dollar spending involved. They render our economy less efficient, and they raise the average level of unemployment.

Another effect of the growing role of government is to introduce increasing rigidity into the price system. The range of prices that are determined freely in the market, that can promptly reflect shifts in demand and supply, has been narrowing year by year. Agriculture is a prime example. The price of agricultural products is cited in many textbooks as illustrating a free market competitive price. That description is now obsolete. The U.S. government fixes many agricultural prices, frequently preventing market forces from either raising or lowering them. Other countries, notably those in the European Common Market, do the same. Restrictions on international trade, such as the U.S. "trigger price" system for steel, effectively shelter a whole range of other prices from market forces. In the United States, many elements limit the flexibility of wages: minimum wages; wage and hour laws; the Davis-Bacon Act, which in effect requires the payment of high union wages on government construction contracts; and special privileges granted to unions. Similar measures exist in other countries, and in many these are accompanied by extensive nationalization of industries, in which all prices and wages are government-set prices and wages. (In the United States, that happens in the postal service and Amtrak.) Some countries control directly a wide range of still other prices and wages—as the United States did from 1971 to 1973.

The recent uproar in the airline industry is an excellent example of how government regulation promotes rigidity. For decades, regulation sheltered the airlines from competition. They could charge high fares without being concerned that new airlines would threaten their monopoly position. The unions of airline pilots, flight attendants, and service personnel were able to capture a generous share of the cartel's profits, thanks to the support they received from government. In *Free to Choose*, we cited George Hopkins, the author of a 1971 study of airline pilots, as concluding, "Today's incredibly high pilot salaries result less from the responsibility pilots bear or the technical skill they possess than from the protected position they have achieved through a union."

Deregulation changed all that. It opened the door to competition. New airlines sprang up, many of them using nonunion pilots and flight attendants, happy to accept jobs at much less than union pay scales. Existing airlines had to lower fares and improve service to meet competition. Fares were based less on what the captive traffic would bear and more on the cost of providing the service. Several airlines went broke, and others sought to renegotiate their union contracts, asking their employees to accept pay cuts. The unions no longer have the field to themselves.

It almost seems as if nobody is happy about deregulation—except the customers, the enterprisers who started the new airlines and their employees, and the economists who preach free markets.

These two aspects of the growth in government's role—the expansion of transfer payments and the growing rigidity of the price system—are, we believe, the fundamental reasons why the level of unemployment has been trending up. They also explain why the unemployment rate remains so intractable. We have heard much about an alleged decline of the so-called smokestack industries—steel, other metals, automobiles, and so on—largely concentrated in the Midwest. They have been subject to heavy unemployment, and there is widespread pessimism about their recovery. Other countries, it is said, have gained a competitive advantage in these industries. In addition, demand has apparently shifted away from their products as light automobiles have replaced heavy automobiles, plastics have replaced metals, and high-tech industries have been capturing a larger share of consumer spending. The ability of the smokestack industries to adjust to the changes in demand is greatly hampered by the rigidity in prices and wages. Although depressed, they are still paying wage rates that are higher than in other industries—*yet the lower paid workers in other industries are being taxed to subsidize the continuance of those higher wage rates.* Despite the publicity about union "give backs" in depressed industries, the extent of adjustment is minor compared to the market pressures, as is evident from the large number of persons who apply whenever there are job openings in these depressed industries.

THE MEANING OF UNEMPLOYMENT FIGURES

Few figures are watched with more fear and trembling than the monthly report on the percentage of the labor force unemployed. The rise from 10.6 percent in November 1982 to 10.7 percent in December 1982 was greeted with dismay and talk about a looming second Great Depression. The subsequent decline to 10.2 percent in January 1983 predictably produced expressions of delight from partisans of the Reagan Administration. The dark clouds of depression were clearing. Yet few figures are more misunderstood, misinterpreted, and misleading.

At its recorded height in December 1982, the actual number of persons recorded as unemployed was 11,628,000. Does this mean, as one might suppose from most news stories on unemployment, that nearly 12 million families are wondering where the next paycheck is coming from? Not at all.

A male breadwinner of the archetypal family of four—husband, wife, and two children—has been out of a job for a year. He is recorded in the statistics as one unemployed person. A teenager, whose father and mother are both employed full-time, is seeking a part-time job while going to school. He or she is recorded in the statistics as one unemployed person. A person has left one job and is waiting to begin another in twenty days. He or she is recorded in the statistics as one unemployed person. On the other hand, the hard-core unemployed person who is not looking for work because he or she is discouraged is not counted as unemployed at all, simply as "not in the labor force." It reminds one of the old story of the restaurateur who, when asked what the recipe was for his specialty, *Hasenpfeffer*, replied that it was half horse, half rabbit—one horse, one rabbit.

Of the nearly 12 million persons recorded as unemployed, nearly 2 million were teenagers, sixteen to nineteen years of age; another

2.5 million were secondary earners in families headed by either a married couple or another male or female; another 3 million consisted of one spouse in families in which the other spouse was employed—this divided almost equally between husbands and wives. Of the remaining 4.5 million unemployed, 3 million were in families in which neither spouse was employed, or in families maintained by one unemployed person. This then leaves 1.5 million either living alone or living with nonrelatives or whose family status was unknown.

Many chief breadwinners are in desperate need of a job. The tent cities that the TV cameras focus on *do* exist and *do* constitute a tragic problem crying for solution. But it is important to have a sense of proportion. Our situation would be dire indeed if nearly 12 million people were potential inhabitants of those tent cities. Fortunately, that is very far from the case.

Look at another dimension of the unemployment figures. Of the nearly 12 million persons recorded as unemployed in December 1982, more than 2.5 million were on temporary layoff or waiting to begin a new job within thirty days. Presumably most of these were receiving unemployment insurance. Another 3.5 million were either persons who were newly entering the labor market or were reentering after having been out of the labor force. About 5 million—or less than half of the total—had lost a job, and nearly a million had left a job voluntarily.

For the most part, unemployment is a brief period between jobs—or between school or housework and a job. Nearly one third of the persons unemployed in December 1982 were either working in the prior month or not looking for a job. At the other extreme, only one fifth, or fewer than 2.5 million persons, had been out of work for more than six months. This is the hard-core group that leaps to mind when we talk about "the unemployed." Their plight is certainly serious—but 2.5 million persons in that position is a far cry from 12 million. Moreover, December 1982 was the worst month. A year earlier, fewer than half as many, around a million persons, had been unemployed for more than six months.

In the course of 1982, many loose comparisons were made between the recession then in process and the Great Depression. These comparisons are extraordinarily misleading. Entirely aside from the major difference in the level of recorded unemployment—more than 25 percent of the labor force at the high point in 1933, compared to 11 percent in December 1982—the character of the unemployment and the economic status of the unemployed were very different. A far larger fraction of the unemployed in the 1930s were hard-core long-term unemployed. Then, there was no unemployment insurance to cushion unemployment, no battery of government welfare and relief programs to help persons who were not eligible for unemployment insurance or whose payments ran out. There were extensive and highly effective private relief and welfare efforts, but the degree of hardship and suffering was of a wholly different magnitude from what is currently true. One set of figures illustrates how far the current situation is from widespread misery. In 1982, the average cash family income in the United States was $26,799. The average income of families with one or more unemployed members was $19,316; of families with members unemployed for more than six months, $18,059.[2]

"JOBS BILLS"

For the past several decades, an almost automatic reflex to a rise in unemployment has been a call for the federal government to "create" jobs. This has been an effective way to expand the scope of government. Each recession has produced government spending programs supposedly as a temporary device to create jobs. But nothing is so permanent as a temporary government program. Those programs have typically moved into high gear only after the economy was on the road to recovery. In the process, they have established an interested constituency that has lobbied for their continuation, thereby contributing to the upward trend in government spending. However effective such programs have been in this respect, they have been utterly ineffective in reducing unemployment—as the upward trend in unemployment demonstrates.

The most recent example is the so-called jobs bill enacted in January 1983—two months after the recession ended. That bill provides for an increase of 5 cents a gallon in the gasoline tax to finance the spending of $5 billion on highway and bridge projects, touted as creating 320,000 jobs. In addition, many of its proponents favor off-setting part of the increased spending on highways and bridges with reduced spending on defense. In fact, the bill will destroy more jobs than it will create.

Financing the rebuilding of bridges, roads, and sewers by spending less on defense creates one set of jobs but destroys another set of jobs. Fewer people would be employed in building tanks, more in rebuilding roads. Perhaps less of the taxpayers' money should be spent on defense and more on bridges—or vice versa. That is a valid and important question about priorities, appropriately decided in a democracy by our elected representatives. But such a reallocation of funds will not create jobs, nor will it reduce unemployment.

Raising taxes to finance job creation actually destroys jobs on net. Taxpayers with less to spend employ fewer people; government employs more people. In addition, higher government spending and higher taxes reduce the incentive for individuals to work, to save, to invest. The direct loss of jobs from lower spending by taxpayers is compounded by an indirect loss of jobs from these supply-side effects. Moreover, the jobs created are government jobs. The jobs destroyed are private jobs. Substituting government jobs for private jobs is hardly the road to prosperity.

Collection of the higher tax started promptly; the repair of highways and bridges will come much later. So, jobs will be destroyed before jobs are created. Finally, the jobs that will be created are primarily high-paid construction jobs—hardly the kind of jobs that will assist the most troubling category of the unemployed, the unskilled and low-skilled.

The jobs go not only to the wrong people but to the wrong places. They go to places that can exert the most political influence, not to those with the highest unemployment. West Virginia is a striking example. It has the highest unemployment rate of any state in the country—approaching 20 percent. Yet it is scheduled to receive only $27 million of the $5 billion total. With more than 1 percent of all the unemployed persons in the United States, it is scheduled to receive one-half of 1 percent of the funds disbursed.

The reason this so-called jobs bill, like earlier ones, was passed is a tale that we have told repeatedly in the course of this book: the benefits are visible, immediate, and concentrated; most of the harm is invisible, delayed, and diffused. People who are employed in rebuilding bridges and highways know that they got their jobs because of a specific jobs bill. People who lose their jobs, or do not get one, because taxpayers spend less or defense spending is lower, *never have the faintest idea that this bill was responsible for their bad fortune.*

One final point that is something of a digression. There is much talk about the deterioration of our "infrastructure"—particularly roads and bridges—and about the difficulty of financing repairs, maintenance, and improvement. These roads and bridges—and the rest of the items included in that fancy word "infrastructure"—were constructed by cities, states, and the federal government when our nation was far poorer than it is today. How is it that we could then afford to build the roads and bridges but cannot now afford to repair and maintain them? This too is a much-told tale: just as the welfare state entitlement programs have been crowding out our capacity to finance defense, so too they have been crowding out the taxable capacity available to finance the fixing of potholes and the repair and rebuilding of bridges, let alone, crucially, the provision of security to persons and property. The traditional functions of government have been starved by the rapacious appetite of the welfare state.

INDUSTRIAL POLICY

The high level of unemployment, the depressed state of the so-called smokestack industries (steel, automobiles, metal fabricating, machine tools) and the electronic revolution have generated a spate of proposals for measures by the federal government to rescue old industries and encourage new ones, measures dignified by the term "industrial policy." As *Newsweek* recently reported, "however homely it may sound, 'i.p.,' as cognoscenti call it, already bids fair to become one of the Democratic buzzwords for 1984."

The name may be new, but the contents turn out to be depressingly familiar: central economic planning to be coordinated by "representatives from government, business [read big business], and labor [read labor unions]," subsidies to the declining industries supposedly to ease their decline, and subsidies to the high-tech industries to foster their growth. All this is to be financed by funds from where? As usual, there is something for everyone except the taxpayer and consumer.

The United States has had an industrial policy since its beginning, and a very successful one indeed, identifiable as free markets, private property, and competition. Though much hindered in recent decades, that industrial policy has continued to operate and to direct industry and labor.

The smokestack industries are said to be declining—we are not certain, in fact, whether they are not simply in a cyclical slump—because of a combination of changing technology, patterns of world trade, high real wage rates that are a carryover from boom periods in these industries, and government regulations and price controls that have reduced their ability to respond to market forces. The "sunrise" industries are expanding because of technological developments produced by private enterprises operating in the market, and because their very newness means that government has not yet been able to render them arthritic by regulations and controls.

The Northeast and Midwest have been declining as employers of labor and the South and West growing because in the former unions have been far more strongly entrenched, and regulations and taxes imposed by state governments have been more onerous. But this regional generalization, though correct, is oversimple. New Hampshire, in the declining Northeast, has kept its taxes low and provided a receptive climate to business. It has also been a low unemployment state. Massachusetts, formerly labeled Taxachusetts, has seen the error of its ways and has reduced tax rates sharply in recent years. As a result, it has shifted from one of the slowest growing and highest unemployment states to one of the fastest growing and lowest unemployment states.

Over and over, pressure on the politician to satisfy every special interest leads government to undertake programs that cancel each other: just as the effect on jobs of extra spending is canceled by the effect of raising the funds to finance the spending. An obvious example is tobacco. Government imposes a heavy tax on tobacco products, thereby raising its price and discouraging smoking. Government subsidizes the growing of tobacco which makes for a lower price, encouraging smoking. Government also finances a campaign by the Surgeon General's office to publicize the harmful effects of smoking and to discourage smoking. Every reader can provide his own further examples of the left hand of government not knowing what its right hand is doing—and there is no reason to be surprised, given the pressure of special interest groups on every side of most issues.

The proposed industrial policy is an egregious example, since self-cancellation is embedded within the one proposal. Technological shifts, as well as other shifts that are always going on in the market, call for the transfer of labor and capital from declining industries to growing industries. The subsidies to declining industries would inhibit this transfer; the subsidies to growing industries would encourage it.

The proponents of industrial policy cite the government bailout of Chrysler Corporation as favorable exhibit Number 1. The government guaranteed a $1.2 billion loan to Chrysler at a time when Chrysler claimed that the alternative was bankruptcy. Subsequently, under the intensely publicized leadership of Lee Iacocca, Chrysler recovered, paid off the government guaranteed loan ahead of time, and the government ended up making a "profit" of over $300 million on warrants to buy Chrysler common stock that had been issued to the government as part of the loan package. Obviously this was a great success, say the proponents of industrial policy—a demonstration of how the government can save an ailing company.

Not so fast. As always, the favorable judgment is reached by looking only at the benefits and not the costs. True enough, the loan guarantee enabled Chrysler to avoid bankruptcy, and, together with other measures Chrysler and its workers took—notably wage concessions by the United Automobile Workers Union—preserved some jobs for Chrysler employees. Those are clear benefits. But what about the costs?

Suppose Chrysler had not been bailed out and had gone into bankruptcy. The Chrysler machines and plants would not have lain idle. A concern that goes bankrupt generally continues to operate under administrators appointed by the court, with instructions to recover as much as they can to meet the obligations that are in default. Many a company emerges from bankruptcy after an interim period to resume full operation as a private enterprise under new management and with a clean financial slate.

Similarly, parts suppliers and the other enterprises related to Chrysler would not have stopped operating. They would have gone on serving whatever Chrysler operations were continued, as well as other automobile manufacturers that inherited the business Chrysler lost. No doubt many of the related enterprises would have suffered losses, along with Chrysler stockholders, but *that is a risk they knowingly ran as investors in order to be able to enjoy profits.*

Even if Chrysler had not continued to operate as a single enterprise, its facilities would not have gone up in smoke or gone to wrack and ruin. If its facilities were worth using to produce automobiles, other automobile companies would have bought and operated them or else new companies would have been set up to acquire them. If Chrysler facilities had not been worth using to produce automobiles but had value for other activities, they would then have been purchased for those purposes. Worthwhile facilities would simply have been taken over by people risking their money in the belief that they could make more productive use of them than Chrysler's management. In the process, they would have created new jobs.

The provision of the loan guarantee to Chrysler did not increase the total amount of capital available to the economy. It simply diverted capital to Chrysler from other uses that the market then regarded as more productive. The market may have been wrong, but there can be little dispute that the market has a far better record than government in judging what are the most productive uses of capital.

Similarly, the provision of the loan guarantee did not increase the demand for automobiles or, especially, for automobiles produced in the United States. If Chrysler sold more cars than it would have under bankruptcy, other automobile companies must have sold fewer. Jobs of Chrysler auto workers were saved at the expense of jobs of workers at General Motors, Ford, and American Motors. There was no net gain here, either.

In our opinion, the major cost of the Chrysler bailout is yet to come. Its apparent success will become an effective argument for the next proposal to bail out a major company in trouble. The taxpayers are not likely to be as lucky the next time, or the next time, or the next time.

Thousands of small companies have failed in the past several years. There were bailout proposals for them—but no bailouts. The reason why Chrysler was bailed out and the many small companies were not is obvious: a concentrated special interest in the one case, diverse interests in the other. And there were no representatives of the persons who were hurt by the bailout! The people who were denied jobs by a Chrysler bailout did not—and do not even now—know who they are. How could they speak out to counter the self-serving claims of Chrysler's management?

The private-enterprise economic system is often described as a profit system. That is a misnomer. It is a profit and *loss* system. If anything, the loss part is even more vital than the profit part. That is where it differs most from a government-controlled system. A private enterprise that fails to use its resources effectively loses money and is forced to change its ways. A government enterprise that fails to use its resources effectively is in a very different position. If Amtrak loses money, it is more likely to get a larger appropriation from Congress than to be forced to change its ways. Indeed, Congress may even instruct it to expand.

An enterprise may, of course, lose money for reasons beyond its control that are not likely to be repeated, or it may lose money because it is mismanaged. If it is possible to tell which, *the market will distinguish*. In the first instance, people who risk their own money will bail the enterprise out of its temporary difficulties; in the second, they will replace the management or force the enterprise to close to preserve assets. Often it is not possible to tell whether bad luck or bad management is to blame. In that case, the market is inclined to act as if it were due to mismanagement. That undoubtedly is harsh on some individuals as well as on some companies. But it is highly beneficial for the community as a whole because it assures that resources are directed toward those enterprises that will use them most effectively.

This system produced the remarkable growth in the productivity of the U.S. economy during the past two centuries. Our increasing rejection of this system in favor of a government-controlled economy is a major reason why productivity in recent years has gone into reverse.

A final word on Chrysler. The defenders of that and similar bailouts counter our objections by pointing to the unfortunate position of the middle-aged skilled automobile worker, whom it is difficult to retrain for other activities when he loses his job. Does he not deserve help? That question does not admit of the straightforward "yes" answer that it seems to call for. Most automobile workers have been earning a great deal more than they can command in other areas of employment. Understandably, they don't like to accept a sharp reduction in their standard of life. You can't blame them. But the question is, should we congratulate them for having been so fortunate in having such remunerative jobs for so long? Or should we impose taxes on people who earn much less than they did in order to enable them to avoid having to take jobs earning wage rates similar to those received by most of the rest of the population? *That* is the real issue. These people, in any event, will not stay unemployed. Most of them have good work habits and skills that are transferable to other industries. There will be many opportunities for them—if not in the automobile industry, or with big companies like General Motors or U.S. Steel, then in the millions of small enterprises throughout the country that now employ the bulk of the labor force. Insofar as workers are in distress, they should, of course, be able to draw on the host of government relief and welfare programs already in existence—like all other residents of the country. But we believe that there is no justification for special measures for the particular benefit of displaced automobile workers.

The Reagan Administration has itself been proposing a new form of industrial policy. It is designed to help the people living in the slums of our major cities. It proposes to establish free enterprise zones to attract businesses to locate in those areas and employ persons who live there; such businesses will be relieved of a wide range of regulations and granted tax concessions and other special benefits. The objective is a fine one, but the plan is a bad one. At best, the proposal would simply shift jobs from outside the slum area to inside the slum area—with the usual discount for the cost of administering the program. In practice, the effect would be worse. We now have a program to favor so-called minority enterprises in granting government contracts. That program has been riddled with scandals. Paper businesses have been set up in which token blacks or token Hispanics are granted formal ownership while control remains in enterprises that could not have qualified for this special preference. Similar things would happen with slum free-enterprise zones. Just what things, we cannot say. We simply do not have enough imagination to figure out all the ways that ingenious people will devise to get a slice of the government's pie.

More basically, we should not designate second-class citizens. Our laws, including regulations and privileges some of us may not favor, should be available for all alike.

PROTECTION

The coincidence of high unemployment and a large so-called deficit in foreign trade has produced major pressure for measures to "protect" American industry from foreign competition—competition that is generally described as "unfair." Here, the Reagan Administration's practice has depar ed from its rhetoric to a greater extent than in almost any other. President Reagan has repeatedly been eloquent in enunciating the case for free trade and against restriction. Yet he has approved one protectionist measure after another—so-called voluntary quotas on imports of Japanese cars, or imports of Hong Kong, Taiwanese, and Mainland Chinese textiles, or specialty steels from Europe; and such other measures as higher trigger prices for steel, a prohibitive tariff on heavy motorcycles for the benefit of a single company, Harley Davidson, and subsidies on the sale of grain to Egypt. On and on.

These measures are one and all ill-advised. They have done little to reduce the trade deficit. They have harmed us all. Many have simply canceled one another. To understand why this is so, we must look first at the basic source of our trade deficit. That source is the increasing instability and insecurity of property throughout the world. Iran and Iraq stay at war; Lebanon and the whole Middle East are in turmoil; there is concern in Europe about Russia's behavior and intentions; the security of property in France is made dubious by a socialist government and in Italy by revolving-door governments as well as high inflation and growing deficits; Mexico is increasingly becoming socialist and is on the verge of bankruptcy; Central America is aflame; Latin American countries face major problems in avoiding economic collapse; and even Canada is imposing onerous burdens on private capital, especially from abroad. In such a world, the United States, for all its problems, is regarded as the safest haven for capital. In addition, it has the most extensive capital markets, the fewest barriers to the acquisition of assets. As a result, capital from all over the world has been pouring into the United States.

How can residents of foreign countries convert the currencies of their own countries into dollars to invest in the United States? To the individual it is simple—if he can surmount the obstacles imposed by his own government, such as the exchange controls recently tightened by the French government. The individual simply buys dollars and uses those dollars to buy stocks or bonds or property in the United States. But where do the dollars come from?

Some dollars may be available from United States residents or enterprises or other holders of dollars who want to invest in the foreign country in question. But that merely offsets the capital outflow, reducing the net capital inflow to the United States. Similarly, some dollars may be available from residents of a country who have received gifts of dollars from relatives or friends, or from the United States government as grants in aid. But again this just reduces the net capital inflow to the United States. Where, then, does the money come from? The major source of dollars is from the sale of goods and services to the United States. A French enterprise, for example, that exports to the United States receives dollars in return but needs francs to pay its workers, taxes, and other costs. Hence it has dollars to sell.

But persons seeking to transfer capital are not the only ones who wish to buy dollars. So also do Frenchmen who want to buy goods from the United States. Only the excess of the dollar value of exports from foreign countries to the United States when matched against the dollar value of their imports from the United States is available for capital export.

Double-entry bookkeeping is a marvelous device. The two sides of a balance sheet, or a cash flow account, must balance. So, too, the total of dollars bought for foreign currencies must equal the total of dollars sold. If many of those dollars bought are in turn used to buy stocks or bonds or other property in the United States, they cannot be used to buy U.S. goods for export. A so-called surplus on capital account—more capital coming in than going out—must be balanced by a so-called deficit on current account—a larger dollar volume of imports than of exports.

Thus, persons living abroad who want to buy dollars to invest in the United States must bid dollars away from persons who want them to buy U.S. goods. In the process they drive up the exchange rate: they drive up the number of francs they are willing to offer for a dollar. This makes U.S. goods more expensive to holders of francs and discourages them from buying U.S. goods. It makes the U.S. market more attractive to sellers of French goods and encourages exports to the United States.

The result has been that the United States has been experiencing a large deficit on current account—misleadingly termed an unfavorable balance of trade—that is mediated through a high exchange rate, that is, a dollar expensive in terms of foreign currencies. One outcry is that the large deficit on current account produces unemployment, that foreign workers are taking away the jobs of American workers. Another is that the foreign capital is attracted simply by high interest rates which, it is said, are the result either of Federal Reserve perversity or the federal government's huge deficits. Both claims contain just enough truth to make them plausible and politically effective, but both are basically false.

True, goods that are produced in the United States and sold abroad mean jobs for U.S. workers. Imports of goods of a kind also produced in the United States mean fewer jobs in those local industries. The agricultural and timber products we sell to Japan mean jobs for U.S. farmers and lumbermen. The automobiles imported from Japan mean fewer jobs for U.S. automobile workers. If the dollars that we spend on Japanese automobiles and other Japanese goods exceed the dollars that they spend on U.S. products, it looks as if there is a net loss of jobs. Not so! Capital imports also mean jobs— of a different kind. The dollars that the Japanese spend on building an automobile factory in the United States also mean jobs in the United States—even though this expenditure is classified as capital inflow and not as current exports. The dollars that Japanese or others spend in buying U.S. stocks or bonds or other assets are not simply squirreled away in safety boxes by the sellers of those assets. They are spent for houses or factories or other items.

It is true that high interest rates attract capital. It is also true that federal deficits tend to raise interest rates. But the capital inflow does not raise interest rates. In fact, it keeps them lower than they would otherwise be. What about deficits? Do they make interest rates go higher? Actually, deficits have in fact been a minor factor in making interest rates high except as they have encouraged the inflationary creation of money.

Suppose we imposed restrictions on imports from Japan and other countries and those countries did not retaliate by imposing restrictions on imports from the United States—the ideal situation in the view of the proponents of "protection." What would happen? As our imports went down, residents of other countries would earn fewer dollars. As a result, they would have fewer dollars to sell, and persons seeking to acquire dollars in order to buy U.S. goods would have to pay a higher price for those now scarcer dollars. That would make U.S. goods more expensive and discourage their purchase. Our imports would go down, but so would our exports. We would "save" one set of jobs; we would "lose" another. The more expensive dollars would make the United States a less attractive place to send capital and so might reduce the capital inflow. That effect might however be minor, since the "safe haven" reason for the capital inflow would still bring in dollars. In any event, the trade balance would improve only to the extent that the capital inflow was discouraged.

In practice, of course, if we impose restrictions, other countries would retaliate. World trade would decline even more, and all of us would be worse off.

To take a specific example, consider the effect of the "voluntary" quotas imposed by the Japanese on the export of cars to the United States in order to "save" the jobs of U.S. automobile workers. Who benefits? Who is harmed? The obvious beneficiaries are the stockholders of the companies manufacturing cars and their workers and suppliers. The obvious sufferers are the stockholders, employees, and suppliers of Japanese auto companies. Also, U.S. consumers now have both a smaller range of choice of cars and must pay a higher price for them. Far less obvious, perhaps the major sufferers are U.S. farmers and lumbermen. Agricultural and timber products are our major export to Japan. If the Japanese now earn fewer dollars by selling cars, they have fewer dollars to buy U.S. products. U.S. exports go down, and all those involved in providing the goods lose. Ironically, the jobs "saved" in the automobile industry are high-paid jobs on the average; the jobs "lost" in the export industries lower-paid on the average. Hence *more* jobs are lost than saved. But, as usual, the jobs "saved" are visible; the jobs "lost" are invisible.

This is another case of the left hand of government not knowing what the right hand is doing. The right hand negotiates the Japanese quotas; the left hand subsidizes agriculture, and these subsidies now increase in order to offset the effect of the quotas.

The self-canceling character of trade restrictions goes much further. Through trigger prices for steel imports—minimum prices below which restrictions on imports are "triggered"—and other protective measures, we make U.S. steel more expensive than foreign steel. But U.S. auto companies use mostly U.S. steel, so their costs are driven up, making them less competitive relative to Japanese automakers. The higher cost of U.S. cars and trucks, thanks to the trade restrictions, in turn raises costs to the steel industry and all other industries. Everybody ends up trying to live at the expense of somebody else.

But what of the plausible argument that if foreign countries subsidize their industries, we must in return subsidize ours, that competition makes sense only on a "level playing field," to repeat the cliché with which businessmen rationalize when they favor free enterprise for others but special privilege for themselves. President Reagan gave an effective answer in one of his speeches when he conjured up the image of two men in a small boat and asked whether, if one of them shot a hole in the boat, the intelligent response by the other is to shoot another hole in the boat. (Unfortunately, in the rest of his speech he announced protectionist measures completely inconsistent with this excellent statement in favor of free trade.) The image is exact. If Japan or the Common Market countries subsidize their steel industry, they hurt themselves and us: they shoot a hole in our common boat. If we, in return, subsidize our steel industry, we increase the hurt to ourselves and to them: we simply shoot another hole in our common boat.

No subject has so united economists since Adam Smith's *Wealth of Nations* was published in 1776 as belief in the virtues of free trade. Unfortunately, with a few exceptions during the nineteenth century, that professional consensus has not prevented one country after another from imposing trade barriers. The special interest of producers has overwhelmed the general interest of consumers. It is a measure of how misleading labels are that, so far as we know, not a single one of the Nader groups that set themselves up as representatives of consumers has occupied itself with the promotion of free trade—*yet restrictions on international trade constitute the most widespread and important burden on consumers.*

CONCLUSION

As noted at the outset of this chapter, the current high level of unemployment has two components: a cyclical component and a long-term trend component. As we write this in October of 1983, the cyclical component has declined sharply as unemployment has declined from 10.7 percent in December 1982 to 9.1 percent in September, and will continue down as the expansion continues. How far down it will go, and when it will reverse direction, depends on the course of the cycle. If, as we fear may prove the case, the expansion ends sometime in 1984, the cyclical component will rise again. Taming the cycle is the only way to reduce these cyclical ups and downs in unemployment. And that requires a steadier, more predictable monetary and fiscal policy.

Continued cyclical expansion will mute some of the loud calls for the federal government to create jobs and some of the complaints about the demise of the smokestack industries and about "unfair" competition from abroad. More important, it will make it easier to resist the calls for subsidy and protection. As expansion proceeds, the smokestack industries will expand along with the rest of the economy; they will recall workers; other displaced workers will find it easier to get jobs elsewhere. Imports will continue to increase but so will the market demand for home-produced goods.

The long-term trend component is a very different thing. Continued cyclical expansion, and even a tamed business cycle, will do nothing to reverse that trend. It is easy to specify the measures that would do so, but hard to get those measures adopted in face of entrenched opposition—the tyranny of the status quo. The major need is to remove or lighten existing obstacles to the free operation of the labor market. What are these obstacles? They are notably minimum wages, Davis-Bacon Act, special treatment of unions, and restrictive regulations on working conditions. They are known. We ourselves have nothing to add on this subject to what we wrote in *Free to Choose*.

The declining importance of labor unions, as a result of the changing composition of employment—away from manufacturing and heavy industries and toward services and high-tech, away from the Northeast and Midwest and toward the South and West—increases the chance of reducing those obstacles. Another reason for hope is that perhaps the few voices among the minority groups who have come to recognize their stake in a freer labor market will multiply and grow in influence. As we have found to be true again and again, *the best ground for hope is the ingenuity and fertility of the market in getting around governmental restrictions.* We have an expanding underground economy that is no respecter of governmentally imposed restrictions. The small entrepreneurs who set up their stands along Fisherman's Wharf in San Francisco, on Fifth Avenue and other thoroughfares in New York, and wherever there are customers to be found demonstrate the strength of market forces, the widespread impulse of people to be independent, to do their own thing.

It is these same market forces that have been reducing the power of unions. The smokestack industries have been declining and the high-tech industries rising only in part because of independent technical change. The higher wages in the smokestack industries to which we have repeatedly referred have reduced their comparative advantage in international trade and have contributed to a better market for the products and services of the high-tech industries. The lesser importance of unionization, the less restrictive state laws, and the generally lower levels of taxation in the Sunbelt, compared with the

Snowbelt, have been far more important than the differences in climate in attracting industry to the one area and repelling it from the other. Deregulation of airlines has freed market forces to operate in that major industry.

It is both an encouraging and a discouraging observation that the ingenuity of people, acting separately, in the economic market in finding ways around governmental restrictions has been far more effective in maintaining a relatively free society than the good sense of citizens acting, jointly, in the political market.

7

CRIME

Lost is our old simplicity of times,
The world abounds with laws, and teems with crimes,

On the Proceedings Against America, *Anonymous, 1775*

THE RISING incidence of crime is surely one of the most troubling problems bedeviling American society in recent years. As government has undertaken more and more responsibilities, it has been performing one of its basic functions less and less well. If the first duty of a government is to defend the country against foreign enemies, the second duty is to prevent the coercion of one person by another and to provide security for its citizens and their property.

We are far richer today than in earlier days. We should be better able to secure person and property than we could when fewer resources were available to the nation. Yet the situation is the reverse. Crime has been rising. The average citizen feels less secure than at almost any time in the past hundred years.

We believe that the growth of government in recent decades and the rising incidence of crime in those same decades are largely two sides of the same coin. Crime has risen not *despite* government's growth but largely *because* of government's growth.

The number of violent crimes of all kinds has literally exploded in the past few decades. In 1957—the first year for which we have data—violent crimes of all kinds numbered 199,000. From then to 1980 they multiplied more than sixfold, reaching 1,309,000. Allowing for the increase in population, the rate per 100,000 persons multiplied fivefold from 117 to 581. Over the same period, crimes against property increased even more rapidly, the rate per 100,000 persons multiplying more than sevenfold from 719 to 5,319.

Over the same period, public expenditures on law enforcement went from $2.7 billion to $25.9 billion, multiplying nearly tenfold. Since prices rose nearly threefold and population rose by one-third, expenditures on law enforcement per capita rose nearly threefold after allowing for inflation. Clearly, throwing money at the problem has been no more effective in curbing crime than in improving education (Chapter 8), or in achieving the fine objectives of the long list of social programs that have been undertaken over those decades. The number of arrests has also risen sharply—from 2 million in 1957 to nearly 10 million in 1980. The rise in the number of arrests simply reflected the rise in the number of crimes committed, not a growing efficiency of law enforcement—the reported number of crimes grew even more rapidly than the number of arrests.

WHY THE INCREASE IN CRIME?

We are not criminologists. Criminologists themselves have no simple and easy explanations of the rapid increase in crime. Nonetheless, some popular explanations can be rejected out of hand, and some partial explanations are highly persuasive.

One popular explanation for crime is poverty and inequality. People are driven to steal, to rob, to murder because they have no other means to avoid hunger and deprivation. Or they are driven to crime because of the spectacle of rich versus poor, a spectacle that feeds a sense of injustice and unfairness, not to speak of the less admirable motive of envy. However plausible this explanation is of why some people turn to crime, it obviously cannot explain the *rise* in crime over recent decades in the United States. As a nation we are wealthier than we were fifty, seventy-five, or a hundred years ago, and that wealth is if anything more evenly distributed. Moreover, there is less poverty and less inequality in the United States than in many other countries. Poverty is certainly more prevalent, more degrading, more intolerable in India than in the United States, and unquestionably the spectacle of rich versus poor is more blatant. Yet, there is less chance of being mugged or robbed on the streets of Bombay or Calcutta at night than on the streets of New York or Chicago.

A closely related view is that the actual degree of poverty or the actual degree of inequality is less important than the *perceptions* of potential criminals, and that those perceptions have been greatly affected in the United States by some of the very technological developments that have been most responsible for the increasing well-being of the population at large, notably in communication and transportation—television, radio, and the like. Television programs, it is said, provide a picture of a life-style that the poor cannot hope to achieve by honest labor, yet is presented as something that everyone has a right to or that everyone can attain.

No doubt such perceptions do contribute to crime. After all, it would be inconsistent to regard the advertising that television carries for products as effective but ignore as ineffective the advertising that it carries for life-styles and moral standards. Nonetheless, we find it hard to believe that a change in perceptions is more than a minor contributing cause of the enormous expansion in crime that has occurred in the past few decades.

Two factors seem to us more important, factors that we have associated in previous chapters with the growth of government in general. One is the change in the climate of opinion, since the time of the New Deal, about the role of the individual and the role of government. That change shifted emphasis from individual responsibility to societal responsibility. It encouraged the view that people are the creatures of their environment and should not be held responsible for their behavior. In its extreme form, the view is that there is no such thing as "crime," that what is called criminal activity is a form of "illness" that calls for treatment rather than punishment.

If people who are poor hold the view that poverty is not their own fault but the fault of society at large, then it is perfectly understandable that their reaction is "Since society is responsible for my poverty, I have every right to act against society and to take what I need or want." Similarly, if they come to believe that the well-to-do whom they see on TV, or observe in high-income neighborhoods, are well-to-do not because of their own efforts—not because they worked hard or saved or in some way contributed to society—but simply because they happened to draw winning tickets in a social lottery, then it is easy to understand their believing that nothing is wrong in correcting the outcome of that lottery by taking property from others.

A closely associated development has been the change in the character of the family. Statistics on divorce, one-parent families, and illegitimate births demonstrate that the nuclear family is losing its traditional role. The family no longer serves as fully as it once did as an integrative institution, as a vehicle for instilling values and developing standards of behavior. Nothing has taken its place. As a result, an increasing number of our youth grow up without any firm values, with little understanding of "right" and "wrong," with few convictions that will discipline their appetites. This is all the more significant, as criminologists have long emphasized, because crime is disproportionately an activity of the young.

Another development that has unquestionably contributed to the rise in crime is the multiplication of laws and rules and regulations. *These have multiplied the number of actions that are crimes.* It is literally impossible for anyone to obey all the laws, since no one can possibly know what they are. Similarly, it is literally impossible for the legal authorities to enforce all the laws equally and without discrimination. To do so, the whole population would have to be employed to police itself. As a result, enforcement of the laws invariably becomes partly a matter of which laws the authorities choose to enforce and against whom—a situation hardly designed to encourage respect for the majesty of the law. We said in *Free to Choose*:

> When the law contradicts what most people regard as moral and proper, they will break the law—whether the law is enacted in the name of a noble ideal . . . or in the naked interest of one group at the expense of another. Only fear of punishment, not a sense of justice and morality, will lead people to obey the law.
>
> When people start to break one set of laws, the lack of respect for the law inevitably spreads to all laws, even those that everyone regards as moral and proper—laws against violence, theft, and vandalism (p. 145).

WHAT TO DO ABOUT IT

Criminologists and others have made many suggestions for altering procedures for apprehending criminals, for indicting them, convicting them, sentencing them, incarcerating them, and so on. Many have urged controlling guns and other weapons to reduce their availability. We have no competence to discuss these proposed remedies. Instead, we can comment only on those aspects of the problem that are tied to our general theme of the importance of reducing government in order to promote the general welfare.

If we are right that the tide is turning, that public opinion is shifting away from a belief in big government and away from the doctrine of social responsibility, then that change will in the course of time tend to alter the circumstances to which we attribute much of the rise in crime. In particular, it will tend to restore a belief in individual responsibility by strengthening the family and reestablishing its traditional role in instilling values in the young.

Moreover, if there is a change in the tide, it will produce some institutional changes that will also contribute to a reduction in crime. In particular, the adoption of vouchers for schooling, as suggested in Chapter 8, could have a major effect. It would offer the disadvantaged who now populate the urban slums greater educational opportunities for their children, giving them a wider and more desirable range of alternatives than street crime. However, any such institutional effects will take a long time to yield their fruits—decades, not years.

One set of changes that could yield relatively rapid results is a reduction in the acts that are regarded by the law as crimes. The most promising measure of this kind is with respect to drugs. Most crimes are not committed by people hungry for bread. By far more are committed by people hungry for dope. Should we have learned a lesson from Prohibition? When Prohibition was enacted in 1920, Billy Sunday, the noted evangelist and leading crusader against Demon Rum, greeted it as follows: "The reign of tears is over. The slums will soon be only a memory. We will turn our prisons into factories and our jails into storehouses and corncribs. Men will walk upright now, women will smile, and the children will laugh. Hell will be forever for rent." We know now how tragically wrong he was. New prisons and jails had to be built to house the criminals spawned by converting the drinking of spirits into a crime against the state. Prohibition undermined respect for the law, corrupted the minions of the law, and created a decadent moral climate—and in the end did not stop the consumption of alcohol.

Despite this tragic object lesson, we seem bent on repeating precisely the same mistake in handling drugs. There is no disagreement about some of the facts. Excessive drinking of alcohol harms the drinker; excessive smoking of cigarettes harms the smoker; excessive use of drugs harms the drug user. As among the three, awful as it is to make such comparisons, there is little doubt that smoking and drinking kill far more people than the use of drugs.

All three actions also have adverse effects on people *other than those who drink or smoke or use drugs*. Drunken driving accounts for a large number of all traffic accidents and traffic fatalities. Smoking harms nonsmoking occupants of the same aircraft, the same restaurant, the same public places. Drug users cause accidents when driving or when at work. According to a recent *Newsweek* article, "employees who use drugs on the job are one-third less productive than straight workers, three times as likely to be injured and absent far more often. . . . Starved, strung-out and coked-up employees affect the morale in the office, scare away customers and hurt the quality of the shirts you wear, the cars you drive and the building you work in."

Whenever we evaluate a government action, we must consider both whether the intended results of that action are ones that it is proper for government to seek to achieve and, further, whether the action will in fact achieve these results. The facts about alcohol, tobacco, and drugs raise two very different issues: one of ethics and one of expediency. The ethical question is whether we have the right to use the machinery of government to prevent individuals from drinking, smoking, or using drugs. Almost everyone would answer at least a qualified yes with respect to children. Almost everyone would answer an unqualified yes with respect to preventing users of alcohol or tobacco or drugs from inflicting harm on third parties. But with respect to the addicts themselves, the answer is far less clear. Surely, it is important and appropriate to reason with a potential addict, to tell him the consequences, to pray for, and with, him. But do we have the right to use force directly or indirectly to prevent a fellow adult from drinking, smoking, or using drugs? Our own answer is no. But we readily grant that the ethical issue is a difficult one and that men of goodwill often disagree.

Fortunately, we do not have to resolve the ethical issue to agree on policy because the answer to whether government action *can* prevent addiction is so clear. Prohibition—whether of drinking, smoking, or using drugs—is an attempted cure that in our judgment makes matters worse both for the addict and for the rest of us. Hence, even if you regard government measures to prohibit the taking of drugs as ethically justified, we believe that you will find that considerations of expediency make it unwise to adopt such measures.

Consider first the addict. Legalizing drugs might increase the number of addicts, though it is not certain that it would. Forbidden fruit is attractive, particularly to the young. More important, many persons are deliberately made into drug addicts by pushers, who now give likely prospects their first few doses free. It pays the pusher to do so because, once hooked, the addict is a captive customer. If drugs were legally available, any possible profit from such inhumane activity would largely disappear, since the addict could buy from a cheaper source.

Whatever happens to the total number of addicts—and the possible increase of that number—the *individual* addict would clearly be far better off if drugs were legal. Today, drugs are both extremely expensive and highly uncertain in quality. Addicts are driven to associate with criminals to get the drugs, and they become criminals themselves to finance the habit. They risk constant danger of death and disease.

Consider, next, the rest of us. The harm to us from the addiction of others arises primarily from the fact that drugs are illegal. It has been estimated that from one third to one half of all violent and property crime in the United States is committed either by drug addicts engaged in crime to finance their habit, or by conflicts among competing groups of drug pushers, or in the course of the importation and distribution of illegal drugs. Legalize drugs, and street crime would drop dramatically and immediately. Moreover, addicts and pushers are not the only ones corrupted. Immense sums are at stake. It is inevitable that some relatively low-paid police and other government officials—and some high-paid ones as well—succumb to the temptation to pick up easy money.

The clearest case is marijuana, the use of which has been becoming sufficiently widespread to mimic the pattern that developed under the prohibition of alcohol. In California, marijuana has become either the largest, or second largest, cash crop. In large areas of the state, law enforcement personnel wink at the growers and harvesters of marijuana in much the same way as law enforcement officials did at moonshiners and bootleggers in the 1920s. Special squads must be set up to fly the helicopters that locate marijuana fields and to make the raids that destroy them, just as in the 1920s, special squads were set up to enforce the prohibition of alcohol. And just as bootleggers had to protect themselves in the 1920s from hijackers, so now the marijuana growers must protect their illegal crop themselves. They post armed guards to protect the growing fields. Gun battles inevitably result, as they did under Prohibition.

Under Prohibition, both bootleggers and do-it-yourselfers producing bathtub gin sometimes used wood alcohol or other substances that made the product a powerful poison, leading to the injury and sometimes death of those who drank it. Currently, the same thing is happening in an even more reprehensible fashion. The U.S. government itself has persuaded some foreign governments to use airplanes to spray paraquat—a dangerous poison—on growing marijuana fields. It has itself done so recently in Georgia. The purpose is to make the marijuana unusable. But there is no way, apparently, to prevent some of the contaminated marijuana from coming on the market and harming those who use it. And there is no certainty that the aim of the helicopter pilots is sufficiently accurate to guarantee that no paraquat falls on plants other than marijuana.

There would be a tremendous outcry if it were known that government officials had deliberately poisoned some of the food eaten by convicted criminals. Surely, it is a far more heinous and utterly unjustifiable practice to spread poison deliberately over crops likely to harm citizens who may or may not be innocent of breaking a law and who have never had their day in court.

Some proponents of the legalization of marijuana have argued that smoking marijuana does not cause harm. We are not competent to judge this much debated issue—though we find persuasive the evidence we have seen that marijuana is a harmful substance. Yet, paradoxical though it may seem, our belief that it is desirable to legalize marijuana and all other drugs does not depend on whether marijuana or other drugs are harmful or harmless. However much harm drugs do to those who use them, it is our considered opinion that seeking to prohibit their use does even more harm both to users of drugs and to the rest of us.

Legalizing drugs would simultaneously reduce the amount of crime and improve law enforcement. It is hard to conceive of any other single measure that would accomplish so much to promote law and order. But, you may say, must we accept defeat? Why not simply end the drug traffic? That is where experience both with Prohibition and, in recent years, with drugs is most relevant. We cannot *end* the drug traffic. We may be able to cut off opium from Turkey—but the opium poppy grows in innumerable other places. With French cooperation, we may be able to make Marseilles an unhealthy place to manufacture heroin—but the simple manufacturing operations can be carried out in innumerable other places. We may be able to persuade Mexico to spray or allow us to spray marijuana fields with paraquat—but marijuana can be grown almost everywhere. We may be able to cooperate with Colombia to reduce the entry of cocaine—but success is not easy to attain in a country where the export is a large factor in the economy. So long as large sums of money are involved—and they are bound to be if drugs are illegal— it is literally impossible to stop the traffic, or even to make a serious reduction in its scope.

In drugs, as in other areas, persuasion and example are likely to be far more effective than the use of force to shape others in our image.

Drug use is not the only area where crime could be reduced by legalizing activities that are now illegal, but it surely is the most obvious and the most important. Our emphasis here is based not only on the growing seriousness of drug-related crimes, but also on the belief that relieving our police and our courts from having to fight losing battles against drugs will enable their energies and facilities to be devoted more fully to combating other forms of crime. We could thus strike a double blow: reduce crime activity directly, and at the same time increase the efficacy of law enforcement and crime prevention.

8

EDUCATION

Each generation of Americans has outstripped its parents in
education, in literacy, and in economic attainment. For the
first time in the history of our country, the educational skills
of one generation will not surpass, will not equal, will not
even approach, those of their parents.

—Paul Copperman, as quoted in A *Nation at Risk*

WE HAVE grown richer over the decades. We have expanded our
knowledge of the universe. "Nonetheless," concludes President
Reagan's National Commission on Excellence in Education in its
report, A *Nation at Risk* (April 1983), "the average graduate of our
schools and colleges today is not as well educated as the average
graduate of 25 or 35 years ago." Has education deteriorated because
we are spending less of our increased income on the education of our
children? Not at all. Expenditures, both governmental and nongov-
ernmental, on elementary, secondary, and higher education have more
than doubled as a percentage of national income since 1929, rising
from 3.8 percent in 1929 to 8.5 percent in 1981. Per pupil expenditure in public elementary and secondary schools (adjusted for inflation) multiplied more than fivefold in the same period (from $395 to
$2,275).

Every poll of parents shows their grave concern about the quality of the schooling their children are receiving. An eight-year study, *A Study of Schooling*, sponsored by the Institute for the Development of Educational Activities, an independent research organization financed by fourteen independent philanthropic organizations, concludes that the American educational system has "deeply entrenched and virtually chronic" problems and should undergo "far-reaching restructuring." The National Commission, similarly, minced no words about how deplorable our children's education is. But agreement about the problem does not extend to agreement on the causes or the solutions.

Television, the breakdown of the family, other cultural changes in recent decades—all have been indicted in examining the poor performance of our public schools. These have undoubtedly contributed to the deterioration in schooling, but they are not the major causes. In our opinion, centralization and bureaucratization of public schooling are the fundamental reasons for the deterioration. As financing of public schools has moved further and further away from local control, the educational bureaucracy has tended to replace parents in deciding what and how our children should learn. The most expedient, and perhaps the only way, to return control to parents is an arrangement whereby parents can choose the schools their children attend and—if they are not satisfied—can move their children from one school to another.

The current debate has focused almost entirely on how poorly our children are being educated. With few exceptions, recommendations for improvement take the present organization of education as a given and do not even consider changing the status quo. A case for government financing of elementary and secondary education can be made on the ground that a democracy can function only if it has a literate, knowledgeable citizenry. That case was strongest during the early years of our nation when immigrants were arriving by the tens of millions and the income level of the majority of the population was low. The case for government financing is far weaker today, when literacy is nearly universal and the majority of the population can afford to pay directly for the schooling of their children if they are relieved of having to pay indirectly through taxes.

Even if it is taken as given that government will continue through taxes to finance elementary and secondary education, *the present organization of schooling should not be taken for granted.* Alternative ways of organizing schooling can give parents greater control over the schooling of their children and thereby introduce competition into schooling. It is significant that higher education has played a relatively minor role in the current debate. Partly, that is because many fewer students are enrolled in colleges and universities than in elementary and secondary schools (only about one-quarter as many). Mostly, however, the reason is that competition plays a larger role in higher education, thanks to the large number of private colleges and universities, and hence the education situation is less dismal than at the elementary and secondary level.

However, even in higher education, the trend has been toward centralization and bureaucratization. The fraction of all students who enroll in governmental—primarily state—institutions of higher education, rather than in private institutions, has been going up rapidly, and so has the financial role of the federal government. Will higher education soon share the fate of elementary and secondary education? What should we do now to improve all levels of education?

During the 1980 presidential campaign, Ronald Reagan singled out education as an area that needed immediate attention. Candidate Reagan advocated four changes:

1. Reduction of federal controls over education. He proposed block grants for education with control to be vested in the states or local communities, and the elimination of requirements for bilingual education.

2. Tuition tax credits to help parents gain some control over their children's education.

3. Elimination of busing for racial desegregation.

4. Abolition of the Department of Education, which had been created as an independent department as recently as September 1979 by President Carter under pressure from the National

Education Association, which has become a major political lobby. President Reagan has made only limited progress in achieving these changes. True, more block educational grants have been made to the states. True, the burdensome and educationally dubious requirements for bilingual education have been repealed, although recently the President has been backtracking on this progress, suggesting that some bilingual education may be necessary. (It is interesting to note that during the period of massive immigration to the country, education in the public schools was in English, not in the language of the immigrant. It is interesting to note further that many educators argue that extensive or prolonged bilingual education results in students not learning *any* language properly.) True, legislation has been introduced for tuition tax credits, but so far Congress has not been willing to enact such credits.

The President's proposal to abolish the Department of Education met such a violent reaction that it was quickly dropped. Instead, reports one of the "Issue Alerts" periodically issued by the White House, "the Secretary of Education has worked to improve the quality of education through speeches, conferences, and other leadership efforts that draw constructive attention to the problem of the schools and offer solutions to the problems"—i.e., lip service, rather than effective action, to reduce the federal government's role in education.

The Secretary appointed the National Commission on Excellence in Education. Its report generated much publicity, but so far has achieved little else. Like much of the literature on schooling, it is long on problems, short on effective solutions. Its recommendations are little more than exhortations to teachers and administrators to do their job better. It confirms, simply, what many parents have known for more than a decade—that their children are not getting a good education. Beyond this, the report's major achievement has been to create an issue for the 1984 campaign.

The two political parties and the two major teachers' unions— the National Education Association and the American Federation of Teachers—are trying to demonstrate their commitment to improving the education of our children. So far, neither has offered much more than good intentions. Here again, we witness the tyranny of the status quo. The unions are back at the old stand: throw more money at the problem, even though the problem has gotten worse as spending on schools has multiplied. The concerned parent can only conclude, bitterly, that politicians are more interested in getting votes, and the unions in raising teachers' salaries, than in improving education. This judgment may be too harsh. Yet, neither the political contestants nor the teachers' unions—nor even the report itself—addresses the crucial issue of why educational standards and achievements have fallen so much in recent decades. In order to improve our children's education, we must first understand why it has deteriorated.

Instead, the Democratic candidates for the presidency accuse the Reagan Administration of neglecting the education of our children by cutting funds for education, and they outbid one another in proposing that the taxpayers fork over still more funds for the school bureaucrats to spend. The Administration bends over backward trying to demonstrate that the President is indeed deeply concerned about the quality of American education. They seek to demonstrate his concern by, among other things, pointing out that "The President's budget for FY [fiscal year] 1984 proposes $4.1 billion for disadvantaged and handicapped children, including $1.0 billion for state grant programs for the handicapped. This is the highest funding level in the history of the program." The same "Issue Alert" goes on to state that, instead of slashing grants and loans for higher education, "The Administration is seeking more Federal assistance for grants and loans in FY 1983. . . . Funding for the Pell Grant program [which provides grants to college students] will increase by $300 million in FY 1984, with maximum grants rising from $1800 to $3000."

The Reagan Administration's reaction to criticism dramatically illustrates how much we are all affected by our environment. The quoted reaction is, almost directly, the opposite of the President's philosophy. He has advocated taking "a serious look at the *true causes of educational decline* rather than resorting to the easy, politically attractive—and historically ineffective—approach of just throwing federal dollars at the problem." He has argued for cutting the extent of government control, not increasing it. When he was governor of California, he proposed that residents of the state—and not just non-residents—pay tuition to attend the state's colleges and universities. Yet he now seems to have succumbed to the tyranny of the status quo.

The report of the commission itself has much to say about symptoms, but little to say about causes. It is full of platitudes. "This report, the result of 18 months of study, seeks to generate reforms of our educational system in fundamental ways and to renew the Nation's commitment to schools and colleges of high quality throughout the length and breadth of our land." Also: "We are confident that the American people, properly informed, will do what is right for their children and for the generations to come." Also: "We must rededicate ourselves to the reform of our educational system for the benefit of all—young and old alike, affluent and poor, majority and minority." Of course.

ELEMENTARY AND SECONDARY SCHOOLS

The report is very clear about how greatly education in public schools has deteriorated. Scores on the College Board's Scholastic Aptitude Test (SAT) demonstrate

> a virtually unbroken decline from 1963 to 1980. Average verbal scores fell over 50 points and average mathematics scores dropped nearly 40 points. . . .
>
> Both the number and proportion of students demonstrating superior achievement on the SAT's . . . have dramatically declined. . . .
>
> Between 1975 and 1980, remedial mathematics courses in public 4-year colleges increased by 72 percent and now constitute one-quarter of all mathematics courses taught in those institutions.

FIGURE 8.1: **Student Aptitude Test Scores: Verbal and Mathematics, 1967–1983**

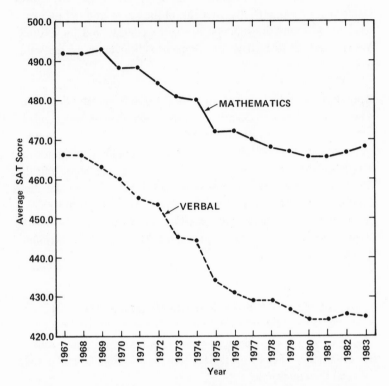

Figure 8.1 documents more fully what has happened to SAT scores over the past seventeen years. The report does *not* stress the vast differences in quality between some public schools and others—public schools in high-income suburbs versus public schools in the inner cities of the nearby metropolises; public schools in small towns versus public schools in large cities. It does not stress the differences in quality between private schools and public schools. Examining the source of those differences would have offered guidance on how to improve the quality of schooling.

During this whole period, expenditures per pupil rose at the state and local levels and even more at the federal level. Total expenditures (adjusted for inflation) per pupil in public elementary and secondary schools doubled from 1960 to 1980. Compared with 1930, they quintupled. A letter to the *Wall Street Journal* (July 25, 1983) illustrates dramatically the change that has occurred over the decades:

> Years ago in Indiana if a pupil in the rural schools wished to enter a public high school he had to pass an examination. In 1910 there were 6,715 rural schools in the state having one room and one teacher and 1,032 having two or more teachers but not having a high school.
>
> What did the state expect the pupil to know? I took the examination in March 1911, and I kept the questions. They cover all of the basic subjects—Geography, Grammar, Arithmetic, Physiology, Reading and History. Here's a sampling:
>
> In what state and on what waters are the following: Chicago, Duluth, Cleveland and Buffalo? State an important fact about each.
>
> Name and locate two countries in which the following are important products: wheat, cotton, wool, coffee.
>
> Write on the Panama Canal, telling who is building it, its location and importance.
>
> What causes the change from day to night, and from summer to winter?
>
> Name five republics, three limited monarchies, and one absolute monarchy.
>
> Name the classes of sentences on the basis of meaning or use. On the basis of form.
>
> Write a sentence with its verb in the active voice; change to passive voice.
>
> What is meant by inflection? What parts of speech are inflected?
>
> Write sentences containing nouns showing six case relations.

Write a model business letter of not more than forty words.

What is the length of a rectangular field 80 rods wide that contains 100 acres?

A wagon is 10 feet long, three feet wide and 28 inches deep; how many bushels of wheat will it hold?

A rope 500 feet long is stretched from the top of a tower and reaches the ground 300 feet from the base of the tower; how high is the tower?

In physiology, name three kinds of joints and give an example of each.

Give the structure of a muscle and of the spinal cord.

Define arteries, veins, capillaries and pulse.

Write a brief biography of Evangeline.

What do you think the author of "Enoch Arden" aims to teach us?

What kind of a man was Shylock?

When I took this examination there was no attempt to pass a pupil so that he could keep up with his "peers." In my days as a college student (I attended four different colleges and universities and received degrees from three of them) I never heard of any institution of higher education giving remedial reading and remedial mathematics.

William H. Bell
Bay St. Louis, Miss.

Answering these questions, today, would baffle a high school graduate or perhaps even a college graduate, let alone a graduate of an elementary school. We venture to say, with regret, that most high school students today would not even understand the questions.

Why have secondary school curricula been "homogenized, diluted and diffused"—as the National Commission asserts? *Why* have standards for graduation from high school and admission to college declined? The report never asks. It recommends that "citizens hold educators and elected officials responsible for providing the leadership necessary to achieve these reforms." But it does not ask whether the current educators and elected officials are not themselves largely responsible for the present situation. Under what motivation, what change of conditions, will they behave differently in the future than in the past?

The commission offers numerous and detailed recommendations:

1. The teaching of English in high school should equip graduates to: (a) comprehend, interpret, evaluate, and use what they read; (b) write well-organized, effective papers; . . .

2. The teaching of mathematics in high school should equip graduates to: (a) understand geometric and algebraic concepts; (b) understand elementary probability and statistics; (c) apply mathematics in everyday situations; and (d) estimate, approximate, measure, and test the accuracy of their calculations. In addition to the traditional sequence of studies available for college-bound students, new, equally demanding mathematics curricula need to be developed for those who do not plan to continue their formal education immediately.

3. The teaching of science in high school should provide graduates with an introduction to: (a) the concepts, laws, and processes of the physical and biological sciences; (b) the methods of scientific inquiry and reasoning; (c) the application of scientific knowledge to everyday life; and (d) the social and environmental implications of scientific and technological development. . . .

4. The teaching of social studies in high school should be designed to: (a) enable students to fix their places and possibilities within the larger social and cultural structure; (b) understand the broad sweep of both ancient and contemporary ideas that have shaped our world; (c) understand the fundamentals of how our economic system works and how our political system functions; and (d) grasp the difference between free and repressive societies. . . .

5. The teaching of computer science in high school should

equip graduates to: (a) understand the computer as an information, computation, and communication device; (b) use the computer in the study of the other Basics and for personal and work-related purposes; and (c) understand the world of computers, electronics, and related technologies.

Fine objectives. But the real question, which the report does not even ask, let alone answer, is how to establish incentives for persons in the educational system to achieve these objectives. The report implicitly accepts the status quo, the present institutional structure as given, the present lines of authority as given, the present methods of governing schooling as given. Their recommendations come down to little more than a pious admonition: "Go thou and sin no more."

Among the recommendations for improving the quality of teaching, the commission recommends that "Salaries for the teaching profession . . . should be professionally competitive, market-sensitive, and performance-based." Market-sensitive salaries are indeed a very effective device for getting good teachers, but only provided there is a market that can be sensitive. *But there is no such market in a socialistically organized system.* As to "performance," who judges competence and how is it determined? Will a poor teacher ever be fired? Look at the experience in the government bureaucracy to find the answer. In public schools, given strong teachers' unions, the situation could become even worse. "Merit" and "performance" are likely to be judged by union officials rather than by parents, or trustees acting effectively on behalf of parents. The National Education Association now opposes proposals for "merit" pay, but that will not prevent it from seeking to take over a system of merit pay if one is adopted.

In our view, the fundamental reason for the deterioration of schooling is increasing centralization and bureaucratization of public schooling. This is a process that has been going on since early in the century, but it accelerated after the 1930s. The number of school districts declined from about 128,000 in 1932 to 84,000 by 1950, and to 16,000 by 1980. Both control and financing of schooling have been transferred from local communities to larger school districts, and then to state departments of education, and recently more and more to the federal government. Professional educators—not parents or students—have increasingly decided what should be taught, how, by whom, and to whom. Monopoly and uniformity have replaced competition and diversity. Control by producers has replaced control by consumers.

Before the 1930s, the federal government played no significant role in elementary and secondary schooling. The states generally left control of the schools to the local community, although a shift toward larger school districts was already in process. Parents monitored schools closely and influenced decisions. The shift in public opinion after the Depression away from self-reliance and local control toward assigning responsibility to government—and later, particularly to central government—produced a rapid shift of power away from parents and local communities. The source of finance for public elementary and secondary schools tells the story. In 1920, local communities provided 83 percent of all revenues, whereas federal grants provided less than 1 percent and the states provided the balance. By 1980, local communities provided only 43 percent of all revenues, states 47 percent, and the federal government 10 percent—a tenfold increase in the federal share, and a near halving in the local share.

Whatever explains the deterioration in the quality of public schools, insufficient spending clearly does not. As we pointed out, spending per pupil doubled from 1960 to 1980. The teacher-pupil ratio rose from 1 teacher per 23 pupils in 1960 to 1 teacher per 19 pupils in 1980. The number of principals and other nonteaching staff multiplied fivefold in those twenty years.

One reason that higher spending has been accompanied by deterioration in the quality of schooling is that the extra spending has not been used to educate our children in reading, in plain and clear writing, and in arithmetic, but to dilute the teaching of the basics in favor of social adaptability, social awareness, and social responsibility. This is not itself reprehensible—unless the three R's are seriously neglected—but it shows a different emphasis from the earlier teaching of history, citizenship, and government (or "civics"). Government and history tend to be viewed as sociology. The National Education Association has distributed to schools 17,000 copies of a curriculum guide dealing with the rise of the Ku Klux Klan—a despicable group—that ends as an indictment of *all* U.S. society. It states: "It is important to remember that the Klan is only the tip of the iceberg, the most visible and obvious manifestation of the entrenched racism in our society." Nuclear arms is another area that the NEA considers appropriate for a curriculum guide in today's schools. This curriculum guide is titled *Choices: A Unit on Conflict and Nuclear War*, and its stated aim is: "To help students understand the power of nuclear weapons, the consequences of their use, and most importantly, the options available to resolve conflicts among nations by means other than nuclear war." Now, a choice ought to be a choice, not a heavily weighted "option."

The shift in curriculum has been accompanied by a decided increase in nonteaching staff. In 1930, classroom teachers accounted for 96 percent of the total staff, principals 3.5 percent, and other nonteaching staff a mere .7 percent. By 1980, teachers accounted for 86 percent of the total and principals 4 percent. Other staff consisting of curriculum specialists, "library/media specialists," guidance and counseling and psychological personnel, and other professional staff had increased to 10 percent.

Will the problems of our public schools be solved by recommendations of the National Commission on Excellence in Education to lengthen the school year, to make mandatory the instruction in mathematics, to impose specific requirements in English, to provide still more funds for public schools? No. These are, at best, Band-Aids. *They do not change the institutional arrangements that determine the incentives of the administrators and teachers in public schools.* The schools are supposed in principle to serve the students—but the students or their parents are almost powerless to influence the character of the schooling. Their only recourse is to operate through the political mechanism, where the status quo reigns. Students and parents play no important role in the educational iron triangle. They are too numerous and dispersed to occupy the corner of this iron triangle reserved for beneficiaries. Instead, that corner is preempted by administrators, teachers, and teachers' unions, who are few and well organized.

The public schools have a captive clientele that typically has no alternative source of schooling except at considerable cost. There is therefore little reason—other than an interest in teaching and doing a good job that fortunately still motivates many classroom teachers— for the administrators or teachers to pay any close and direct attention to the needs or criticisms of students or parents. They have a far more immediate incentive to concentrate on getting higher pay, smaller classes, and fewer hours of work, which can be accomplished better by the standard political techniques of lobbying and campaign contributions, rather than by doing a better job teaching.

You cannot make a dog meow or a cat bark. And neither can you make a monopolistic supplier of a service, one that does not even get its funds directly from its customers, pay close attention to its customers' wants. The only way to do so is to break the monopoly, to introduce competition, and to give the customers alternatives. That is why, as we pointed out in *Free to Choose*, the "way to achieve a major improvement, to bring learning back into the classroom, especially for the currently most disadvantaged, is to give all parents greater control over their children's schooling, similar to that which those of us in the upper-income classes now have" (p. 160). We spelled out in some detail a plan for educational vouchers that would assure parents greater freedom to choose schools for their children while retaining present sources of finance.

Under such a plan, parents receive vouchers corresponding to all or part of the amount that the state or local community is committed to spending to provide public schooling for their children. These vouchers can be used only for schooling. In its simplest form, vouchers are usable at public as well as private schools, and the vouchers are the only source of funds for the public schools. In other versions, public schools receive funds not only from vouchers but also directly from the state or local community. In still others, vouchers are usable only at private schools.

None of these versions alters the source of government funds for schooling. As now, all citizens, whether they have children or not, and whether they enroll their children in private or public schools, would pay taxes to finance government expenditures on schooling. The key difference, and it is crucial, is that parents—and not government bureaucrats—would decide what schools their children attend. In the process, they would also decide which schools got more funds and which less, and parents who chose private schools would be relieved, at least in part, from having to pay twice for schooling their children—once through taxes, once through school fees. The result would be to give teachers and administrators a strong incentive to meet the wants of their real customers—the students. "The customer is the boss" is the characteristic slogan of a competitive market. Vouchers would make that slogan apply to schooling.

The desperate search by many parents for alternatives to public schools is persuasive evidence of the difference that a voucher system could make. Among other results, that search has led many non-Catholic parents to enroll their children in Catholic parochial schools—the only private schools they could afford because the parochial schools are heavily subsidized by the Catholic Church. It has also led to a rise in the percentage of all students enrolled in private schools, despite rising fees.

Tuition tax credits—that is, allowing parents to deduct part or all of the fees that they pay to a private school from the income tax that they would otherwise pay—is a member of the same family of reforms as a full-fledged voucher plan. Like vouchers, such credits introduce a greater measure of competition and widen the choices available to parents. However, in the form in which they are generally proposed, they are only a partial and unsatisfactory equivalent to universal vouchers. The reason is that they are usable only by parents who have income tax liabilities, and usable in full only by parents whose income tax liability is greater than the maximum credit allowed. The most disadvantaged parents, whose incomes are so low that they pay little or no income tax, get no benefit whatsoever.

That defect can be remedied by making the tuition tax credit transferable. That is, a person subject to tax but having no children could pay the tuition of someone else's child and take a corresponding tax credit. Since the cost to the taxpayer of providing the benefit of the credit to an indigent family would be zero, and since the total amount of tax liability is a large multiple of the total usable tuition credits, essentially every needy child could get the benefit of the credit. Transferable tuition tax credits would then become the equivalent of a universal voucher equal in amount to the maximum tax credit.

In the past, a major obstacle to introducing a voucher plan has been the church-state issue. The Supreme Court has generally ruled against state laws that provide assistance to parents who send their children to parochial schools. That obstacle may have been removed by a Supreme Court decision on June 29, 1983, upholding by a 5 to 4 vote a Minnesota law permitting tax credits for tuition and other payments made by parents of children in private or public schools. This is the first time that the Court has approved a statute that provides tax relief to parents who send their children to private schools and that does not exclude church-run schools.

While removing one major obstacle, the Supreme Court decision by no means guarantees success for the voucher idea because, as Senator Packwood said, "At bottom, the opposition has been philosophical and the Supreme Court's decision did not change those who philosophically opposed the concept." A far greater obstacle is the opposition of the education bureaucracy, which will not willingly turn control of the schools over to competition. As Willard McGuire, president of the National Education Association, said, "Tuition tax credits, in whatever form they may appear, divert badly needed tax resources from the (public schools)."

As parents have become more and more discouraged about the education of their children, support for the voucher plan has grown. In 1979, the Education Voucher Institute was established as a nonprofit organization to serve "as a clearinghouse for dissemination of information related to expanded choice and [to] provide publicity, publications, speakers and sponsor seminars to further this goal."

Attempts to conduct voucher experiments have been made in

several states, but so far with little success. The educational bureaucracy has been effective in stymieing every such attempt. In 1978, supporters of vouchers in Michigan succeeded in getting an initiative on the ballot to establish a voucher system. While it was defeated, it was favored by 26 percent of the voters—a respectable showing for a first try. In California, a move is on to qualify an initiative that would require the state to give every child residing in the state a state voucher to be used "to pay for instruction, supplies, facilities, and other services or equipment provided by schools entitled to accept vouchers in grades Kindergarten through twelfth."

The most encouraging sign is from a recent Gallup poll, which for the first time recorded a slim majority of respondents (51 percent) in favor of a voucher system. A fascinating feature of the poll is that approval of vouchers was highest among black respondents (64 percent)—the group we believe would benefit most from a voucher system. Recognition that there is an alternative to our present inadequate system is clearly spreading rapidly. As it spreads, it will create irresistible pressure for change.

HIGHER EDUCATION

A growing percentage of young people in recent decades have been going to college. And a steadily increasing fraction of them are enrolling in governmentally run institutions—currently nearly 80 percent. The private schools that led in fostering quality education in the United States are finding it more and more difficult to compete for students, and for funds, with government institutions. It is difficult to attract paying customers when you are selling something that is being given away by government.

In the 1930s, before government's role in education began to accelerate, enrollment was evenly divided between private and governmental institutions—about half a million students in each. Even in 1960, there was not a great difference, about 1.5 million in private institutions, somewhat over 2 million in government institutions. But over the next twenty years, enrollment in government institutions more than quadrupled, to 9.5 million, while enrollment in private institutions less than doubled, to 3 million. It is a tribute to the quality of the private institutions that they were able to increase their enrollment, let alone double it, in face of the far lower tuition charges in government institutions. Nonetheless, the uneven competition had its impact. In the decade of the seventies, more new government institutions were established than private institutions, *but six times as many private institutions closed their doors.*

Government institutions have been growing rapidly not only in number but also in size. Complaints are common about the impersonality of the mega-universities; it is alleged there is a neglect of the individual student, a standardization and routinization of the educational process. Though nearly four times as many students are enrolled in state colleges and universities as in private colleges and universities, private schools are still more numerous than state schools, with the result that private schools remain relatively small and more personal.

Spending by the federal government on higher education has been growing at an ever-increasing pace: from $200 million in 1960 to $1.25 billion in 1970 to $5.5 billion in 1980—a more than tenfold increase in twenty years even after correcting for inflation. Over the same period, state and local spending on higher education quadrupled after correcting for inflation. These developments raise two separate issues: First, should there be any government subsidy for higher education? Second, if there is a subsidy, how should it be distributed?

The present use of tax monies to subsidize higher education seems to us one of the great suppressed scandals of our day. The young men and women who go to college on the average come from higher-income families than those who are not in college—yet both sets of parents pay taxes. And, whatever the income of their parents, those young men and women will occupy the higher rungs of the economic ladder. Indeed, *we doubt that there is any other government program that so clearly and so massively transfers income from relatively low- to relatively high-income classes.* We in the middle-income classes in effect have conned the poor into supporting us in a style that we take to be no more than our just deserts.

Do impecunious parents whose children do not go to college or the children themselves benefit from having their more affluent neighbors' children go to college? No issue that we raised with the seven young people who took part in our recent TV discussions engaged their interest so deeply as this one—for obvious reasons. Most of them were studying at or had graduated from private not government institutions, yet they recognized that they were beneficiaries of government spending on education and were not accustomed to seeing themselves depicted as "fat cats" battening on the poor. Like most young people, they are idealistic and would not willingly play that role. On the contrary, as we have discovered frequently in other discussions with students, they are prepared to adopt positions hostile to their narrow interests if they are once persuaded on grounds of principle.

Some students in our discussions argued that the government was justified in taking money from the impecunious people whose children were not going to college in order to subsidize young people who were fortunate enough to go to college because everyone would benefit "by having a more educated society." They found it hard to accept the view that the students themselves, not society, were the primary beneficiaries. When we cited the example of Henry Ford and other innovators as having benefited society, and asked whether they too should have been subsidized by the taxpayers, they were bemused by the analogy.

The views of these students are shared by many, especially those who benefit from the government's (i.e., the taxpayers') largesse. Ronald Reagean's attempt as governor of California to require all students at state colleges and universities to pay tuition succeeded only in arousing the animosity of the university community. The situation remains the same today. Fees have increased in recent years but the fees are limited to supporting student services such as counseling. The Board of Trustees of the California State University System recently voted on a report from its finance committee recommending the removal of restrictions on the use of student fees, in order to allow them to be used to help pay classroom costs. The trustees voted to keep the restrictions because having students pay any part of the expense for their schooling would be against the policy of the state. The Board of Trustees apparently agrees with our students.

It is eminently desirable that every young man and woman, regardless of the wealth or religion or color or social standing of his or her family, have the opportunity to get whatever schooling he or she can qualify for, *provided that he or she is willing to pay for it— either currently or out of the subsequent higher income that the schooling will make possible.* There is a strong case for assuring the availability of loans or their equivalent, by governmental means, if necessary. There is no case that we can see for providing subsidies.

Since, however, as in so many other instances that we have stressed in this book, the persons who benefit are well aware of what they would lose if government subsidies were removed and are very vocal—whereas the persons who pay and do not benefit are less aware of how much they are paying and are less vocal and more easily conned—the situation will undoubtedly remain as it is for some time. Therefore, we shall go on to our second issue: given that there is a subsidy, however large or small, how should it be distributed?

Currently, we distribute the subsidy primarily by having the government run institutions of higher learning and by charging tuition to students that is far below the costs incurred on their behalf. This is both inequitable and inefficient. Moreover, it is this practice, even more than the subsidization of higher schooling, that promotes conformity and threatens individuality.

Under current arrangements, the State of California says to its young men and women, "If you meet certain academic standards, we shall automatically grant you a scholarship worth thousands of dollars a year regardless of 'need'—provided that you are smart enough to go to one of the state colleges or universities. If you are so perverse as to want to go to a private university like Stanford or Harvard or Yale or the University of Chicago, not a penny for you." Surely, it would be more equitable to proceed instead along the lines of the

G.I. educational benefits for veterans. Let whatever money the State of California wants to spend on higher schooling be divided into the appropriate number of scholarships, each of, say, $4,000 per year (the approximate expenditures in 1981 of all state institutions of higher education in the United States per person enrolled), such scholarships to be tenable for four years. Let there be a competitive exam—or some other method of selection—and let these scholarships be awarded to individuals to be used to attend any approved institution of their choice that will in turn accept them. If California wants to continue to run its universities and colleges, let those institutions charge tuition sufficient to cover the costs, and compete on even terms with other institutions. If they are more attractive to students than other institutions, they will flourish; if not, they will decline.

Today, there is no reason for faculties and administrators of the existing state institutions to pay any attention to their students, except as this will indirectly affect the legislature which votes them funds. The thing for them to do, as they well know, is to engage in activities that will appeal to the legislature while paying to students the minimum attention that will keep them from being too obstreperous. In all too many cases, the way to appeal to the legislature is to apply the most lenient possible academic standards to the classroom performance of athletes.

The arrangement we suggest gives students a wider range of choice and enables them to exert more influence on the kind of schooling they are offered. It eliminates the present unfair competition between state-run and other institutions.

It gives the faculties and administrations of state-run institutions an incentive to serve their students, much as a voucher system does in elementary and secondary education. It opens up the opportunity for new institutions to enter the field and seek to attract customers. The strengthening of competition would promote improvements in quality and foster diversity and experimentation. Because the money would go to individuals, not institutions, it would be clear who are the recipients of the subsidy and bring into the open the question of who *should* be subsidized. Also, it would give individuals greater freedom of choice, greater opportunity to express their own values and to develop their own capacities as effectively as possible.

All of these are advantages of the scholarship plan. But they are also, to speak cynically, the major political obstacles to its enactment. As usual in such matters, the people who would benefit from the change do not know that they would. The vested interests that have developed under the present arrangement will recognize the threat to them at once.

CONCLUSION

The present ferment about education will undoubtedly produce major changes. The question is not whether changes will occur, but rather what kind of changes? Will these changes simply strengthen the status quo, the present stranglehold of professional educators on the most important socialist institutions in our society—elementary and secondary public schools and government colleges and universities? Or will real changes in those institutions through a voucher system or tuition tax credits or some other device give parents greater choice of the schools their children attend? We believe that introducing competition can alone lead to a major improvement in the quality of schooling available to all strata in our society.

Unfortunately, the omens are not propitious. The political reaction has been to call for more of the same. Reports are pouring out of the educational establishment in response to the public outcry. And those reports have been conforming to the same pattern as the report of President Reagan's National Commission on Excellence in Education—simply accepting the present institutional structure but urging boards of education, principals, and teachers to do different things and do them better, and dropping crocodile tears over the costs involved in improving the educational system.

The real solution is very different. Private schools often provide far better education than governmental schools at half or less than half the cost. Schools are no exception to the generalization that anything government does tends to cost twice as much as it costs if done in the private market. The real issue is not higher spending but putting the consumer—the parent and the child—in the saddle.

9

THE IRON TRIANGLE: HOW TO DEFEAT IT

What effect we wish our acts to have does not come into the question in considering the consequences of those acts. What we are concerned with is the natural consequences of our acts and not the motives which prompt them.

Simon Newcomb (1885)[1]

THE UNITED STATES has made some progress since the election of Ronald Reagan in 1980 in satisfying the desires of the majority of the citizenry for a smaller and less intrusive government. If progress has often seemed slow, and sometimes backward, we can comfort ourselves with the thought that the same tyranny of the status quo that makes rapid progress difficult will also make it difficult to undo the progress that has been made. The question remains how we can speed up the process, how we can more effectively translate the public will into governmental policy. This book offers a number of clear lessons that can help us to do so.

1. The strongest political influence on a legislative body is exercised by special-interest groups of citizens who favor a government program that confers substantial benefits on them, while imposing small costs on a large number of their fellow citizens. Each such group

is a corner of an iron triangle of beneficiaries, politicians, and bureaucrats.

2. A corollary is that we cannot correct this situation by electing the "right" people to Congress. Once elected, the "right" people will do the wrong things. And they will be pressured to do so by us, in our capacity as members of special-interest groups, even though we elect them in our capacity as members of a majority outraged by the growth in government's spending and scope.

3. Only two routes exist whereby the general interest can express itself, whereby a package deal can be arranged in which we accept cuts in "our" programs because we recognize that we would gain more from cutting "their" programs than we would lose by the cut in "ours." One route is via the presidency; the other is through Constitutional Amendment.

4. The President and the Vice President are the only federal officials elected by *all* the people. They are the only ones who have a political incentive, once elected, to put the general interest above sectional interests. One route to curbing government is therefore to elect a President committed to that task.

5. The presidential route is easier than the Constitutional route but ultimately less effective. A newly elected or reelected President dedicated to making major changes will have a visible effect on government policy only during an initial honeymoon period of six to nine months. Thereafter, the tyranny of the status quo asserts itself. The iron triangle which is the form of the status quo will succeed in stymieing further changes and will produce some reversals of initial changes. However, the visible changes will continue to exert invisible effects for a long time.

6. To halt an exploding federal government, truly, and cut it back to size will, we believe, require taking the Constitutional route. That was the experience of the Framers of our Constitution when the Articles of Confederation generated trends threatening the very existence of the United States of America. The Framers found that a Constitutional Convention and the adoption of a new Constitution were the only effective ways to rectify matters. In doing so, they for-

tunately included a provision whereby the public at large could directly influence the Constitution in addition to relying on indirect influence through Congress. Article 5 requires "The Congress, . . . on the application of the Legislatures of two-thirds of the several states . . . [to] call a convention for proposing amendments." Any such amendments, like those proposed by the Congress, must be ratified by three-fourths of the states to become effective.

7. The Constitutional route is now being taken. The greatest progress so far is with respect to an amendment that would require Congress to balance the budget and limit taxes. Prodded in 1982 by calls from thirty-one of the necessary thirty-four states for a Constitutional Convention to propose a budget-balancing amendment, the Senate passed an excellent amendment by the necessary two-thirds majority. The House approved the amendment by a majority but short of the necessary two-thirds vote. Since then, a thirty-second state legislature (Missouri) has called for a Constitutional Convention, increasing still further the pressure on Congress to give the citizens in the fifty states an opportunity to approve the amendment—as they would do promptly, once given the chance. Prospects are good that other states will soon join the bandwagon.

8. The most promising long-run strategy to limit government is to adopt the same route for other key Amendments, notably Amendments

(a) to give the President an item veto;

(b) to replace the present so-called progressive income tax by a true flat-rate tax;

(c) to require the federal government to keep the increase in the quantity of money it issues to a low fixed rate year in and year out.

* * * * *

Mao Tse-tung is reported as having said that a long march starts with a single step. In the United States we have taken that step and are on our way—fortunately, in the very opposite direction from Mao's. This land is blessed in having to surmount only one tyranny: that of the status quo. And we are equally blessed in a vigorous, energetic, and public-spirited populace that is more than equal to that task. There is nothing wrong with the United States that a dose of smaller and less intrusive government will not cure.

NOTES

CHAPTER 2

1. Milton Friedman, "Tax Follies of 1970," *Newsweek*, April 27, 1970.
2. From Robert E. Hall and Alvin Rabushka, *Low Tax, Simple Tax, Flat Tax* (New York: McGraw-Hill, 1983), p. 3.
3. Alexander Hamilton, James Madison, and John Jay, *The Federalist Papers* (1788), ed. Clinton Rossiter (New York: New American Library, 1961), no. 45, p. 291.

CHAPTER 3

1. Quoted in C. Northcote Parkinson, *The Law and the Prophets* (Boston: Houghton Mifflin, 1960), p. 93.
2. Thomas Hazlett's interview with Philip Gramm, *Manhattan Report* (Manhattan Institute for Policy Research), vol. 1, no. 7, October 1981, p. 7.
3. Jeremy Bentham, *Defense of Usury; Shewing the Impolicy of the Present Legal Restraints on the Terms of Pecuniary Bargains* (1787). Reprinted in *The Works of Jeremy Bentham*, Bowring edition (Edinburgh, William Tait, 1839), Part IX, p. 17.
4. James T. Flexner, *George Washington: The Forge of Experience (1732–1775)* (Boston: Little, Brown & Co., 1965), p. 211.
5. William Safire, *Before the Fall* (New York: Doubleday & Co., 1975), pp. 249–50.
5a. The discussion of a Constitutional Amendment to balance the budget and limit spending draws heavily on Milton Friedman, "Washington: Less Red Ink," *The Atlantic*, February 1983, pp. 18, 20–24, 26.

6. *New York Times*, June 11, 1976, p. A16.

7. Hall and Rabushka, p. 4.

8. Ibid., p. 19.

9. Commissioner of Internal Revenue v. Newman, 159 F.2d 848, 850–851 (2d Cir. 1947); Helvering v. Gregory, 69 F.2d 809 (2d Cir. 1934).

CHAPTER 4

1. Parkinson, pp. 64, 91–93.

2. Sheldon Richman, "Capitol Offenses," *Inquiry*, vol. 6, No. 8, July 1983, p. 48.

CHAPTER 5

1. Milton Friedman, "More Double Talk at the Fed," *Newsweek*, May 2, 1983, p. 72.

2. Quoted from the text of the resolution. The substance of the resolution was later incorporated in the Federal Reserve Act in the form of an amendment to the act passed in late 1977. See Robert E. Weintraub, "Congressional Supervision of Monetary Policy," *Journal of Monetary Economics* 4 (April 1978): 344.

3. Milton Friedman, "Congress and the Federal Reserve," *Newsweek*, June 2, 1975.

4. James L. Pierce, "The Myth of Congressional Supervision of Monetary Policy," *Journal of Monetary Economics* 4 (April 1978): 369.

5. *Report to the Congress of the Commission on the Role of Gold in the Domestic and International Monetary Systems*, March 1982, vol. 1, p. 21.

CHAPTER 6

1. *Second Thoughts on Full Employment Policy* (London: Institute of Economic Affairs, 1975), p. 129.
2. Estimates provided by John F. Cogan, Associate Director, U.S. Office of Management and Budget.

CHAPTER 9

1. *Principles of Political Economy* (New York: Harper & Bros., 1885), p. 532.

ACKNOWLEDGMENTS

LIKE OUR EARLIER BOOK *Free to Choose*, this book is linked to a TV series scheduled to be broadcast in 1984 under the title "Tyranny of the Status Quo," which consists of three half-hour discussions between Milton Friedman and seven young people, six of whom are graduate students at various institutions, one a recent graduate.

We are indebted to William Jovanovich for suggesting the book— and, in conjunction with it, the TV series. Robert Chitester, the executive producer of "Free to Choose," was also the executive producer of the new TV program. He has become a friend and ally in our efforts to present to the public ideas on how to preserve and extend our free society. Richard Vigilante, himself a participant in the television discussions, helped to select other participants. The talented young people who participated in the discussions held widely varying views on a broad range of topics, and they improved our own understanding of differing attitudes on central issues. We are indebted to David Brooks, Steve Calabrese, Harry Crocker, Gary Jenkins, Lee Liberman, and Carola Moen.

Finally, with respect to the manuscript, our greatest debt is to William Jovanovich, whose substantive suggestions improved both the contents and exposition. Aaron Director, David Friedman, and Janet Friedman read the whole manuscript and made many useful suggestions. Michael Boskin, John F. Cogan, D. Gale Johnson, and Rita

Ricardo-Campbell generously provided key items of information. We were fortunate also to have Marianna Lee as our editor at Harcourt Brace Jovanovich.

The book would never have been ready in time except for the efforts of Gloria Valentine, who typed successive drafts and provided skilled research assistance. It is a level of performance we have come to expect from her—far above and beyond the call of duty.

INDEX